CONSCIOUS COLORING

BRINGING YOUR MIND INTO PLAY

COLORABLE ARTWORK BY CATHY LYNN

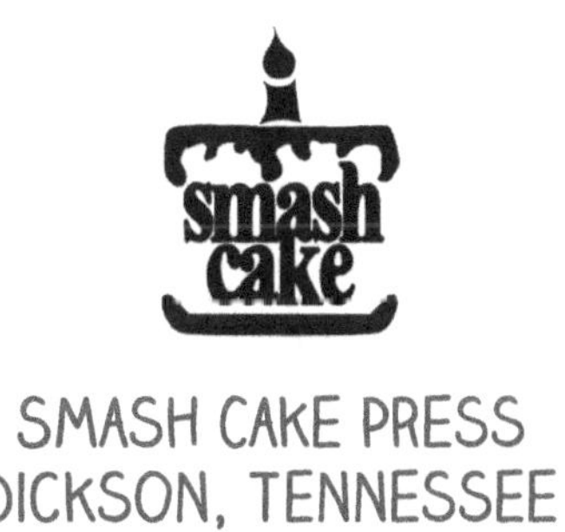

SMASH CAKE PRESS
DICKSON, TENNESSEE

Smash Cake Press
P.O. Box 1756
Dickson, TN 37056-1756
www.smashcakepress.com

ISBN-10: 0996660704
ISBN-13: 978-0-9966607-0-9

First printed edition, September 2015

Printed in the United States of America on acid-free paper.

The publisher and artist wish to thank their friends, both online and off, for providing such thoughtful feedback and support during the creation phase of this project. You guys are the best. We also wish to acknowledge in particular our friend and colleague Mike Turner, who suggested the title we ultimately chose.

Bulk discounts for ten books or more are available upon request.

THIS BOOK IS DEDICATED TO MY PARENTS

FOR THEIR EXPRESSED BUT SOMEWHAT UNFULFILLED

CREATIVE SOULS. I LOVE AND MISS YOU.

SPECIAL THANKS TO TRACY LUCAS

FOR MAKING THIS BOOK A REALITY.

Cathy Lynn

HOW TO USE THIS BOOK:

Each piece in this book is hand-drawn. Some will appear twice; those are included in both a larger and smaller size. None of the images were digitally created, so they are intentionally not "perfect." There will be anomalies, wavers, and perfectly beautiful imperfections in each one. And even though they began as my drawings, they will become yours through the way you choose to enhance them, using color (or the lack of color!) to make parts of each picture stand out in a way that is pleasing to you.

THE FIRST RULE OF THIS COLORING BOOK IS THAT THERE ARE NO RULES.

This is ***your*** playground, and there is no wrong way to let loose. Relax, settle in, and use this book in whatever way unlocks you. That's the whole point! If you'd like, though, here are some suggestions.

TOOLS:

To avoid bleed-through, we recommend sliding a piece of heavy cardstock between the pages if you're using instruments like markers, pens, or paint to color your book. Another option is removing the page you're interested in and putting it on a cheap clipboard before you get to work. (Sometimes, using the same paper or clipboard over and over results in a whole new kind of art itself!) Also try mixing tools; marker shaded with colored pencil, maybe, or light watercolors layered beneath metallic permanent markers. Experiment!

VISUALIZATION:

If one of the drawings strikes you in a way that relates to something you want to bring into your life, color it as you focus on your vision. That could be finding a resolution to a certain conflict, having the freedom to express your true creative self, or even acquiring a material thing like a new home. Anything goes. See your vision through the colors you choose. Use the act of coloring as a way to bring your vision into the world in a tangible way; then display the piece somewhere to help you stay focused on your vision.

MEDITATION:

Pick a palette of colors. You might decide that various shades of blue are what you want to work with, or the rainbow order, or all pastels. See what fits your mood. Then, color mindfully. And only color – no multitasking. Focus on the curve your strokes fall into, on the sound your hand makes across the page, on the way the colors blend or contrast. Let your mind become completely engrossed in this act of coloring in such a complete way that nothing else enters your head. And if any mental clutter sneaks in, acknowledge the thought and notice it; then put it aside and go back to focusing on the colors and the drawing at hand, rather than following the train of thought down a rabbit hole. Keep coming back to the colors you're using, the way they fill the spaces between and around the lines of the drawing, the tactile sense of what you're experiencing now, in this one moment. Let everything else slide away for a while. You might be amazed how refreshing this exercise can be, even if you only have a few minutes to spend at a time.

AFFIRMATION:

Some of the drawings in this book have thoughts, phrases, or ideas within them. Choose a page that you want to work with as an affirmation. If you find that none of the preprinted wordings work for you at this moment, choose another drawing that speaks to you and fits with the affirmation you want to work with. Pull your colors intuitively as you focus on the intent, think about it, and affirm it positively. Color your page, and think about the affirmation – the way you'll feel when it becomes a part of your everyday life, and what the result will mean to you. Then write your wording within, beneath, or even on the back of the piece of art you've created. When you're finished, hang your work somewhere prominent. Feel that affirmation every time you look at it, and remember the truth in it. Let your creative work bring that positivity or goal to mind on a daily basis.

TWIST THE IDEA:

Anything you can hold in mind, you can play with using this medium. Focus on whatever best suits your own needs. We've seen colorists use these to represent a motivational quote, a dream, a rich childhood memory, a favorite song, or even a character in a manuscript. Several of these pieces were drawn while I worked through a period of intense grief and disruption. Getting lost in the creative process was one of my ways of coping with the overwhelming feelings of sadness. Perhaps that could work for you, as well. You could also color while concentrating on a spiritual thought or verse, or to capture the essence of someone you care about (who might even like to receive it as a gift.) If it feels right, try it!

RESPECT YOUR ART:

It doesn't matter that you didn't actually draw these pieces. The lines on these pages are simply lines – guides, if you will — for you to use, color, enjoy, and work with to create something that is uniquely you and uniquely yours. No one else will put the exact same colors, flourishes, and choices as you will into these drawings. When you complete a piece, own that, and enjoy it! Frame the page, hang it, or put on the fridge with a magnet. You might even slide it into the cover of a three-ring binder, if you have the kind with a clear front pocket. However you choose to preserve or display your work, look at it and know that you and only ***you*** created that coloration, that specific feeling, that beautiful spark. That's huge! Be proud!

SHARE YOUR WORK:

The publisher and I created this book for you because we truly adore coloring. We have actually colored many of these same drawings ourselves –and we LOVE to see how others have used them. It's amazing to see how many different ways people can bring themselves forth, even when we all started from the same blank piece! So please, please, please feed our passion for these images and share your art with us. You can even tell us what you were visualizing, affirming, or thinking about as you colored, if you're comfortable doing so.

UPLOAD YOUR COLORED IMAGES AT:

Artist's page: facebook.com/artistcathylynn

Publisher's page: facebook.com/smashcakepress

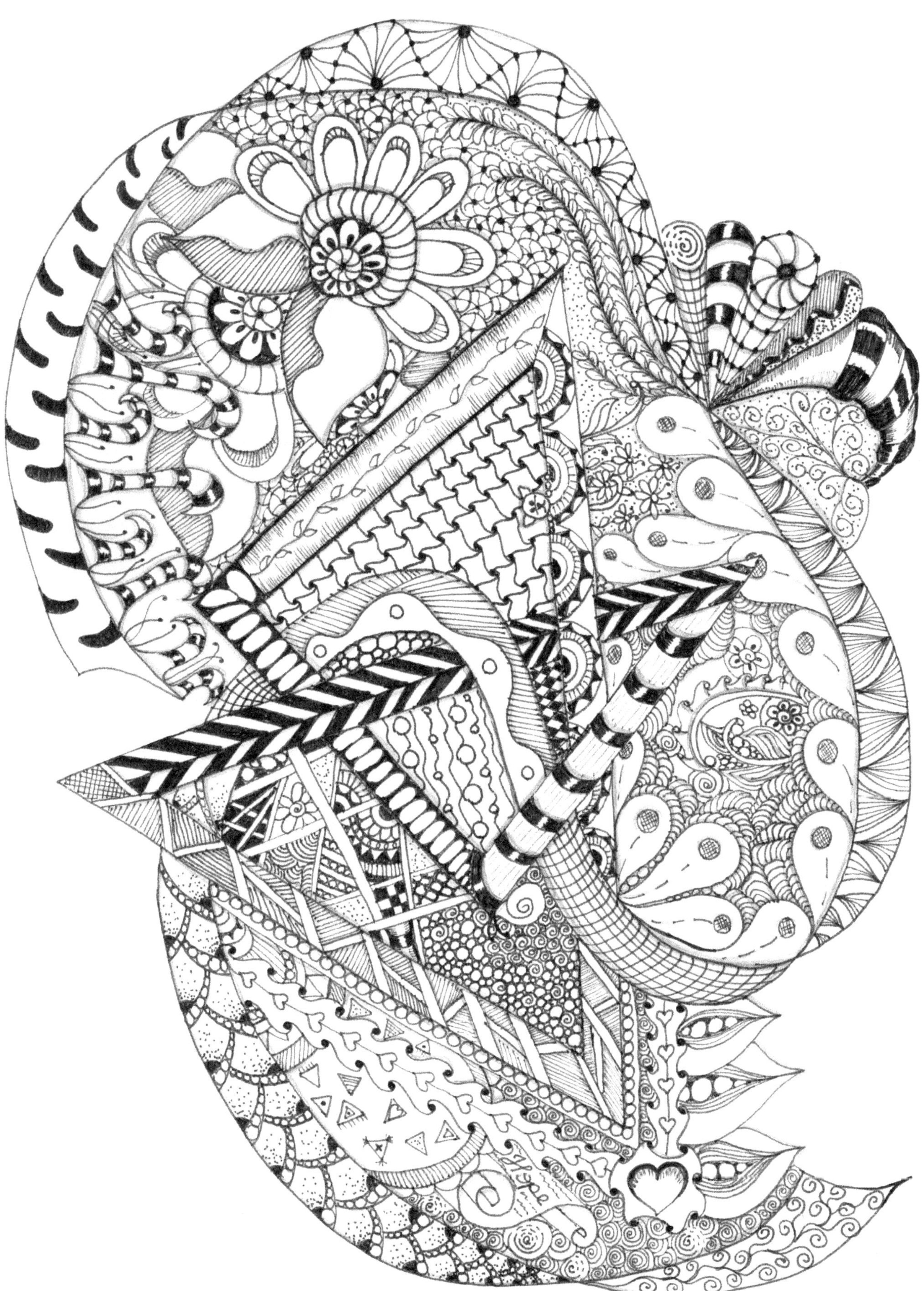

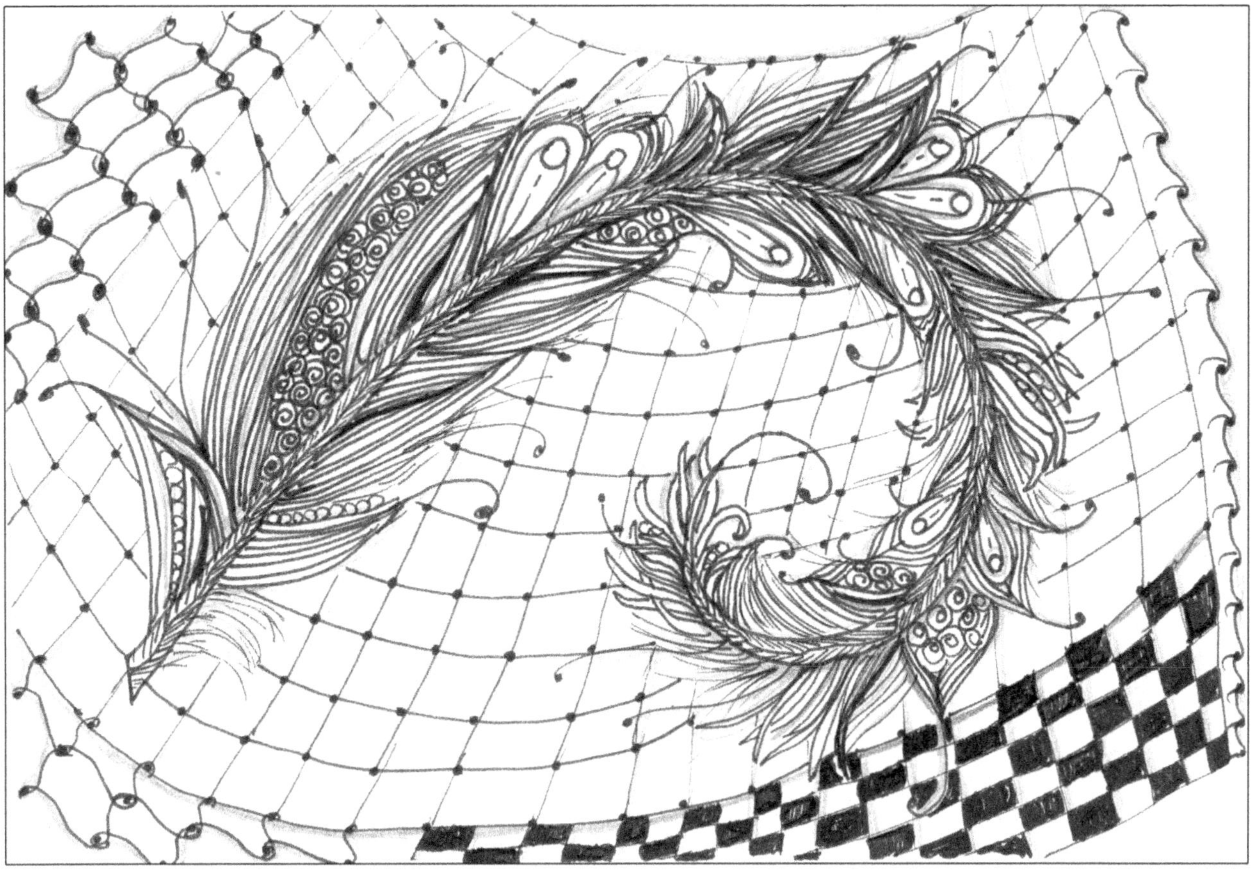

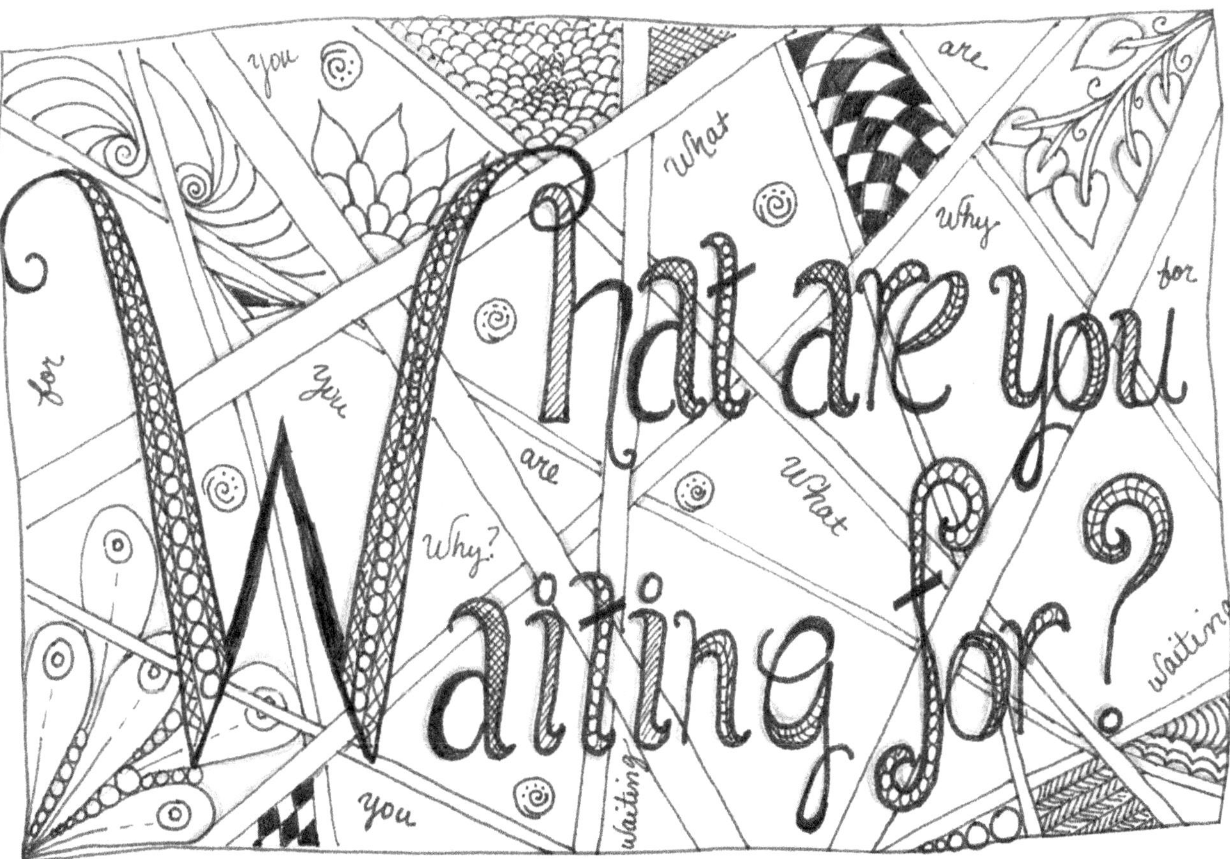
What are you Waiting for?
you
are
What
Why
for
for
You
are
What
Why?
waiting
you
waiting

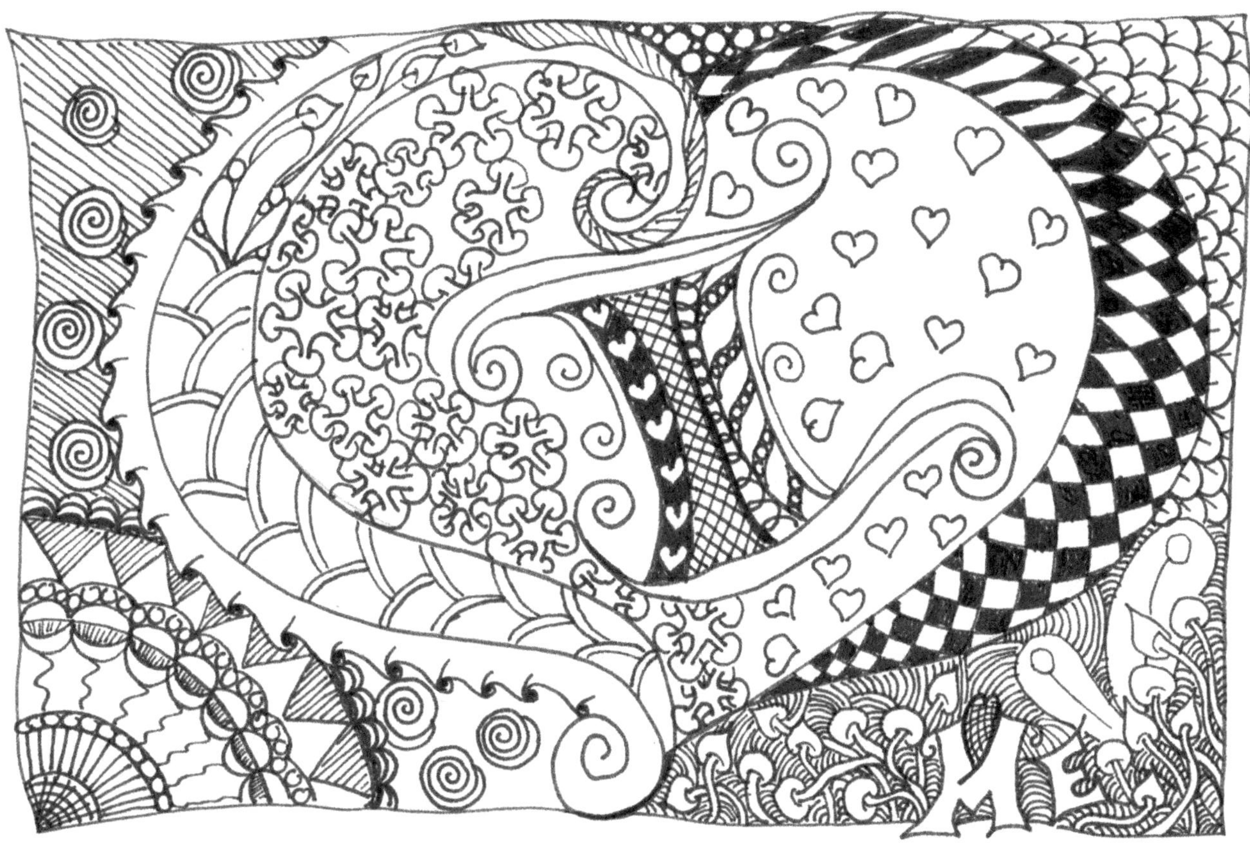

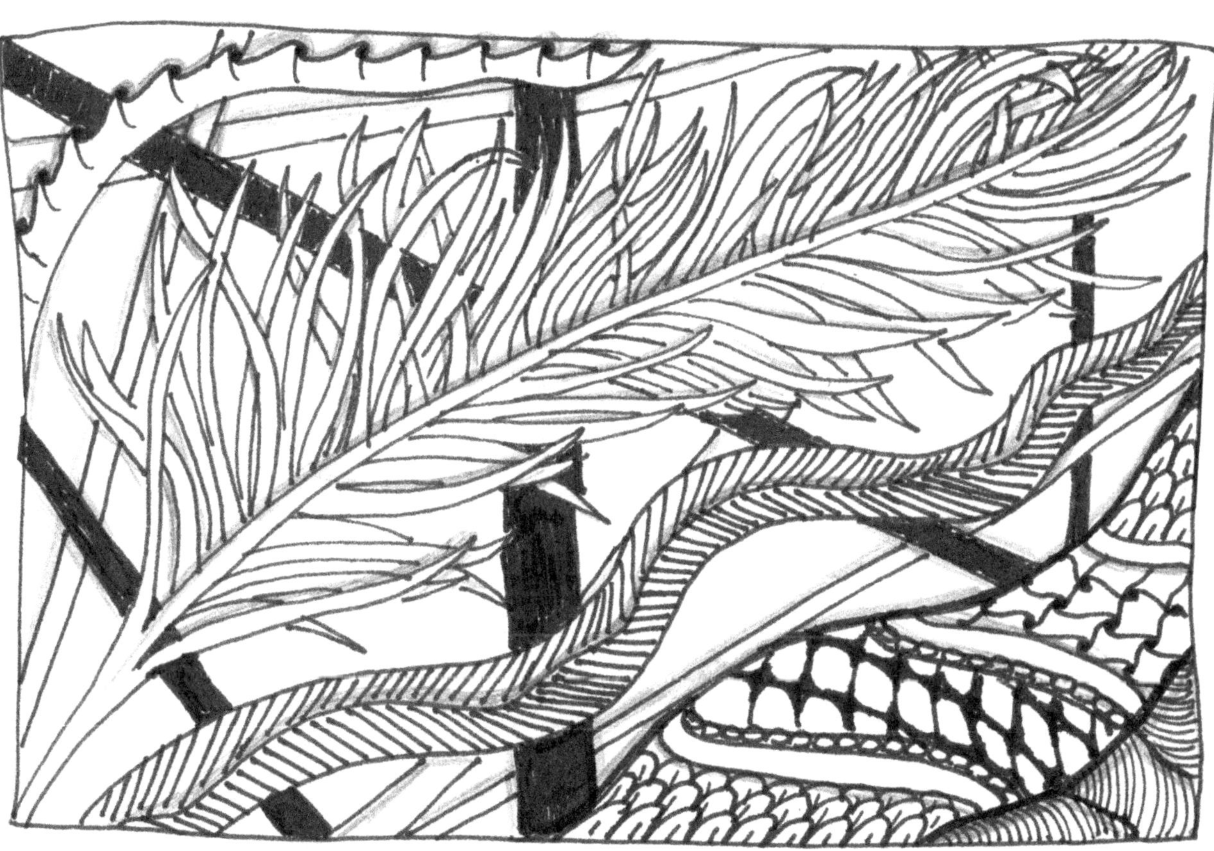

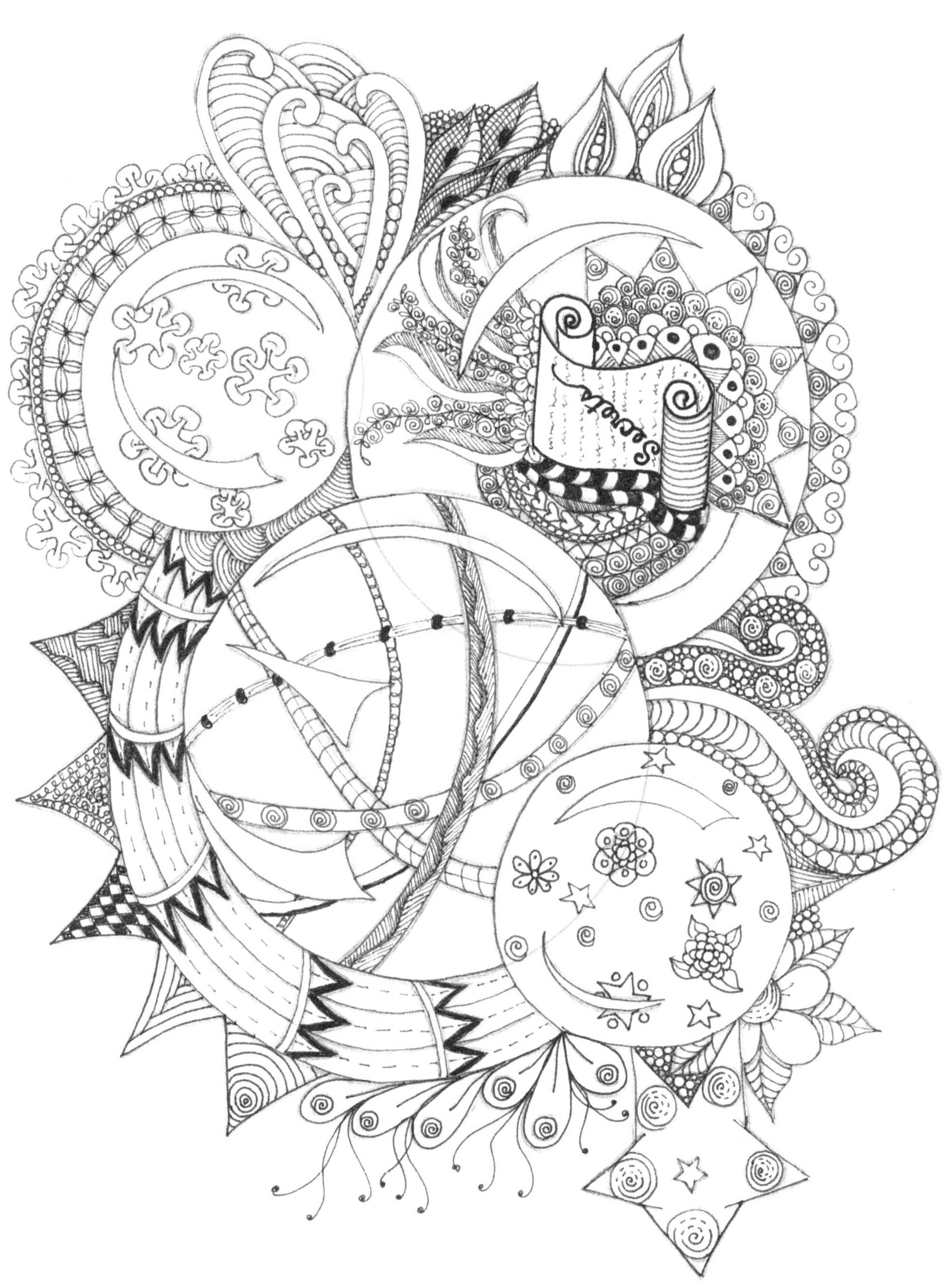
Secrets

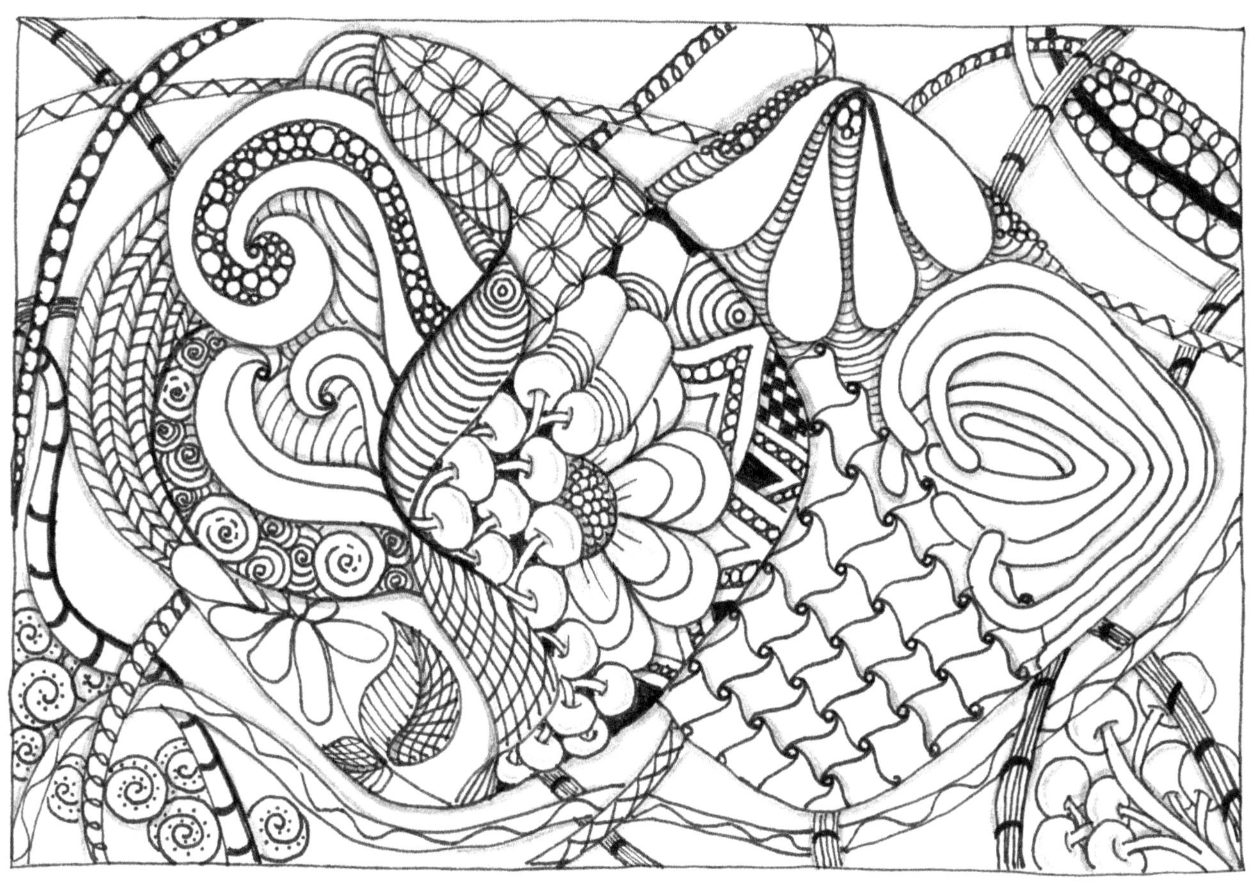

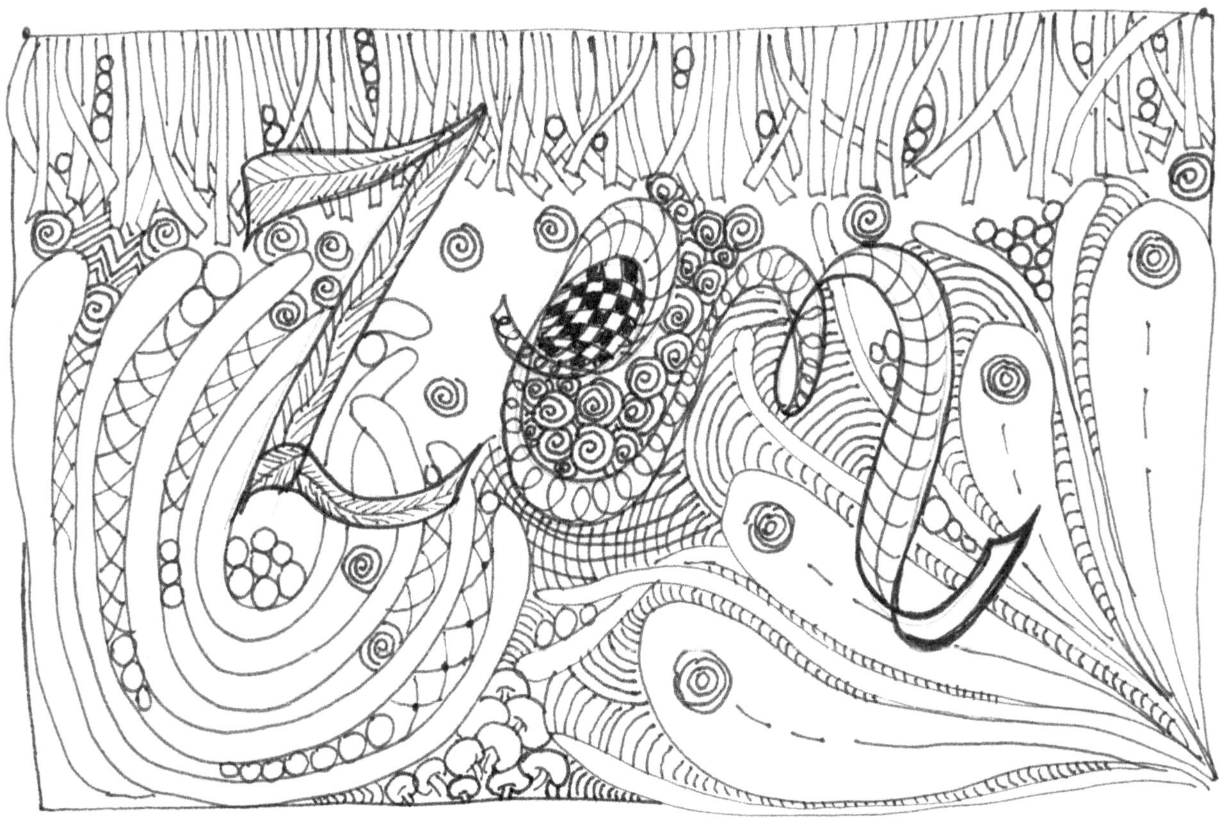

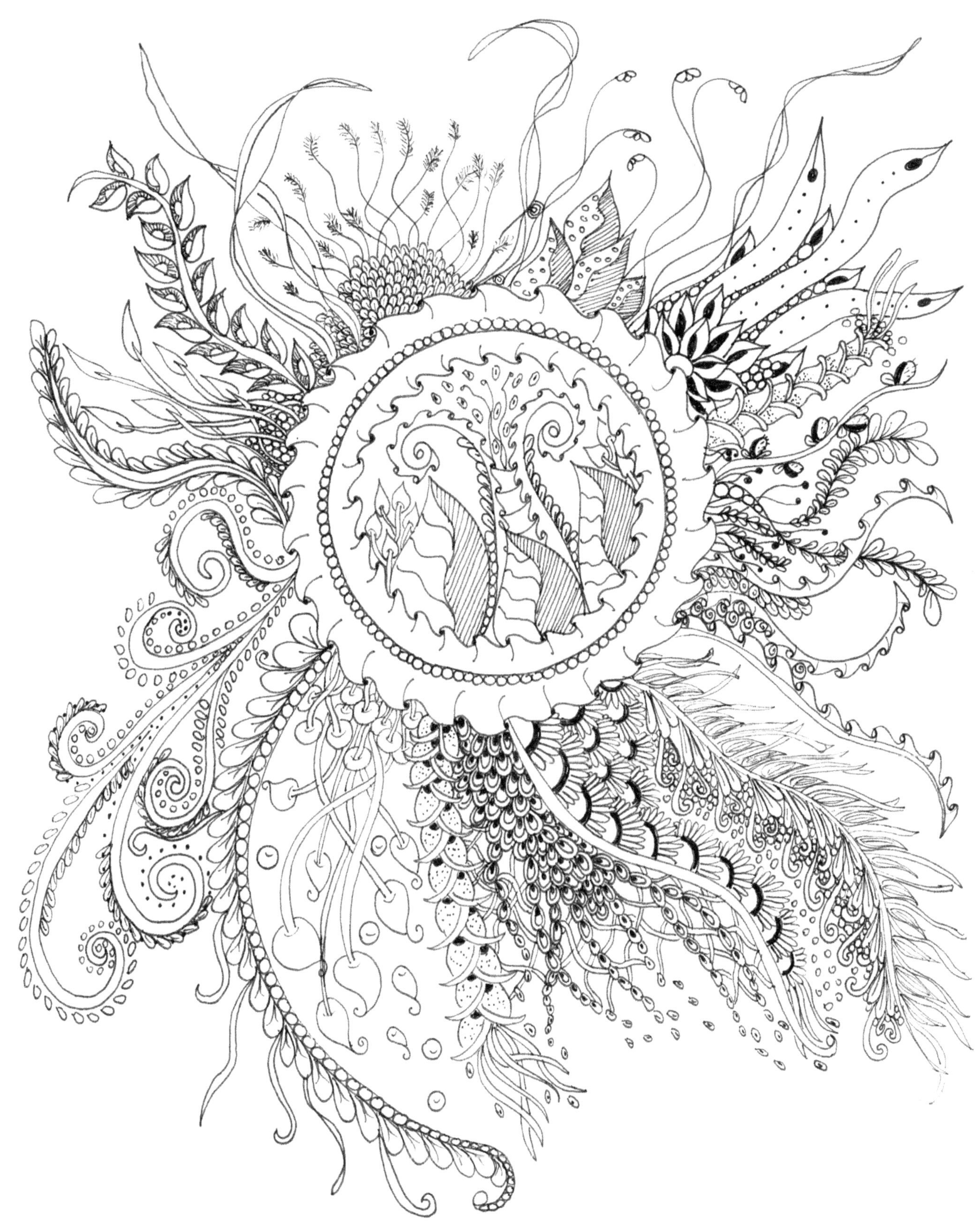

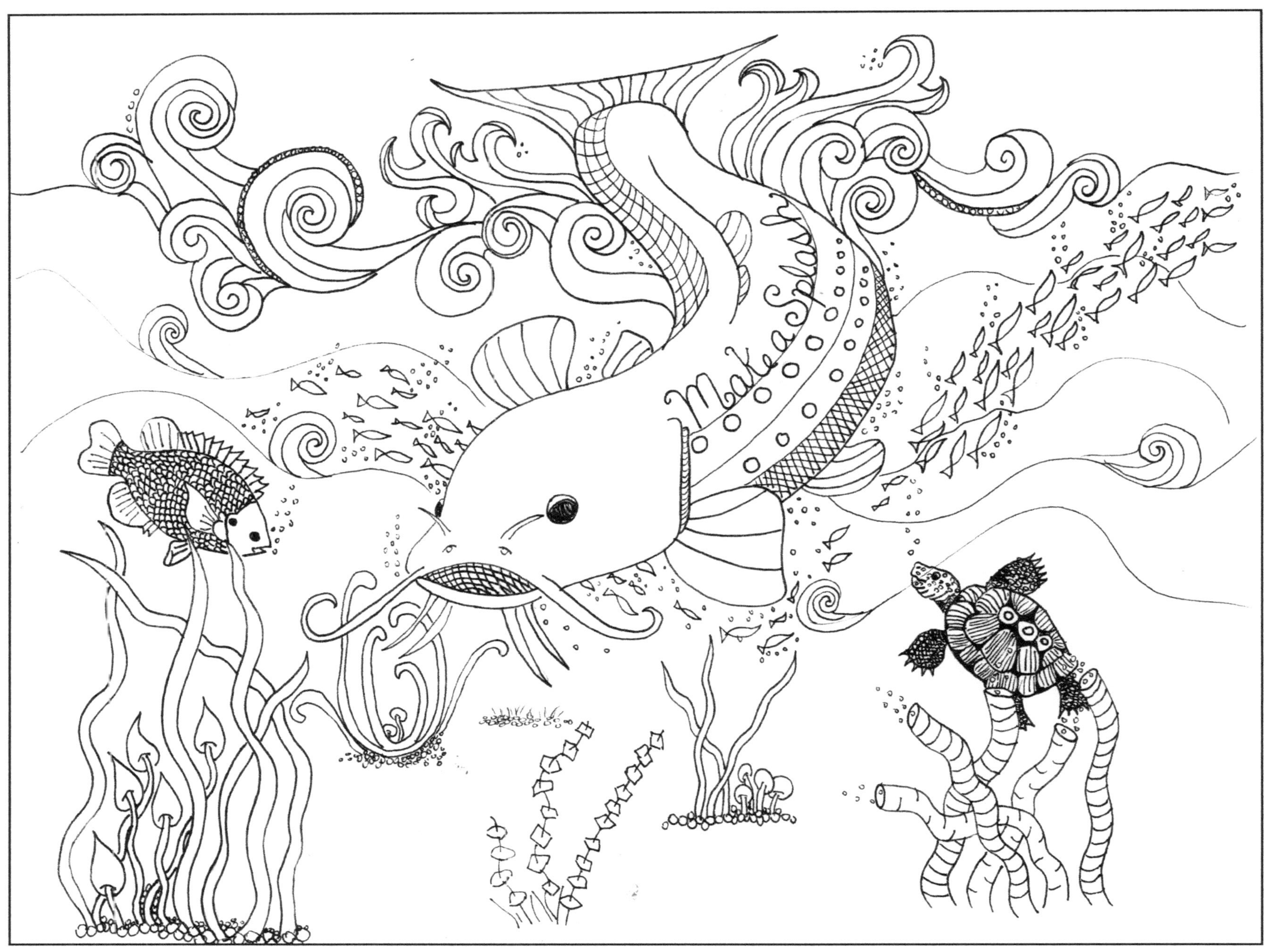
Make a Splash

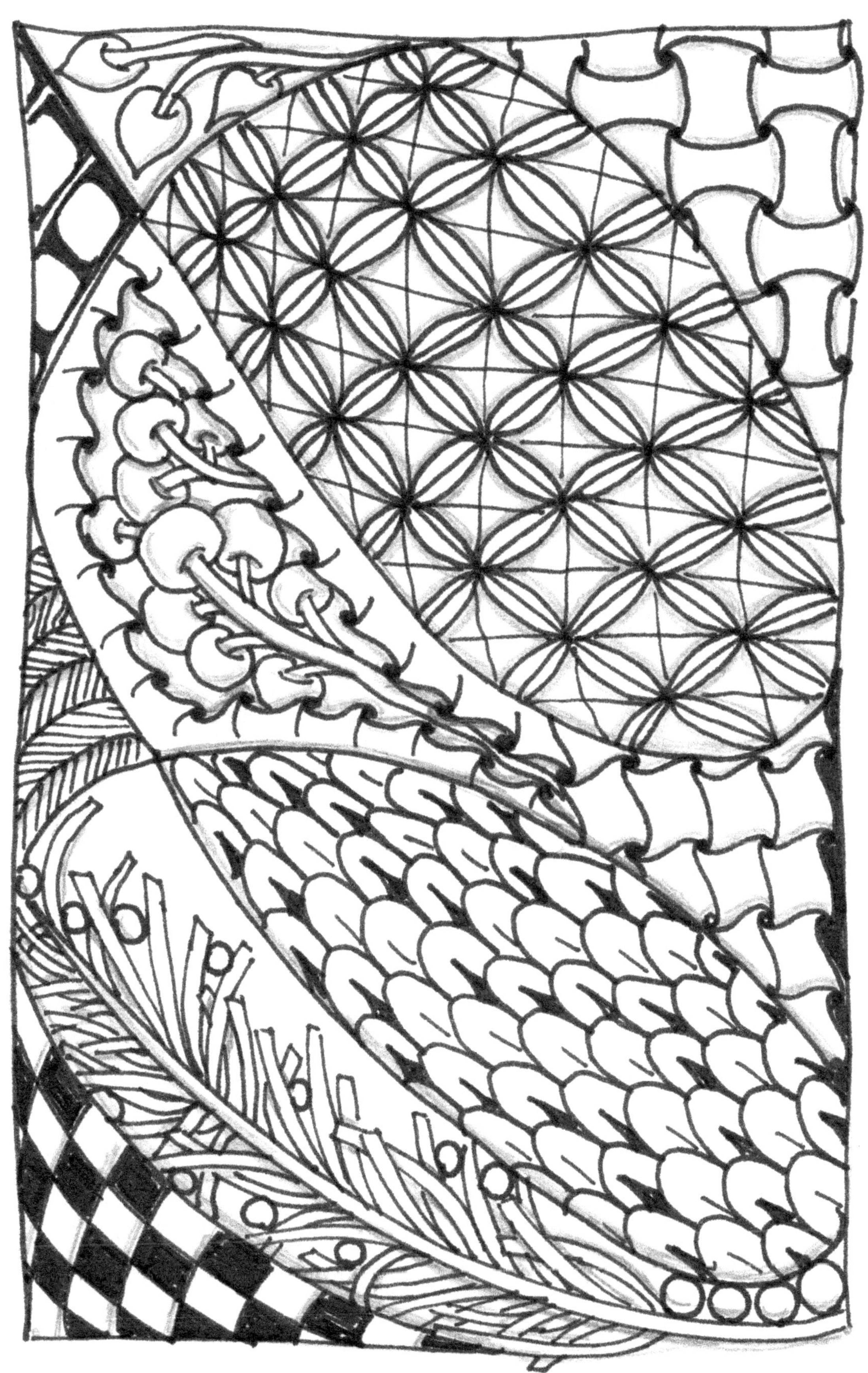

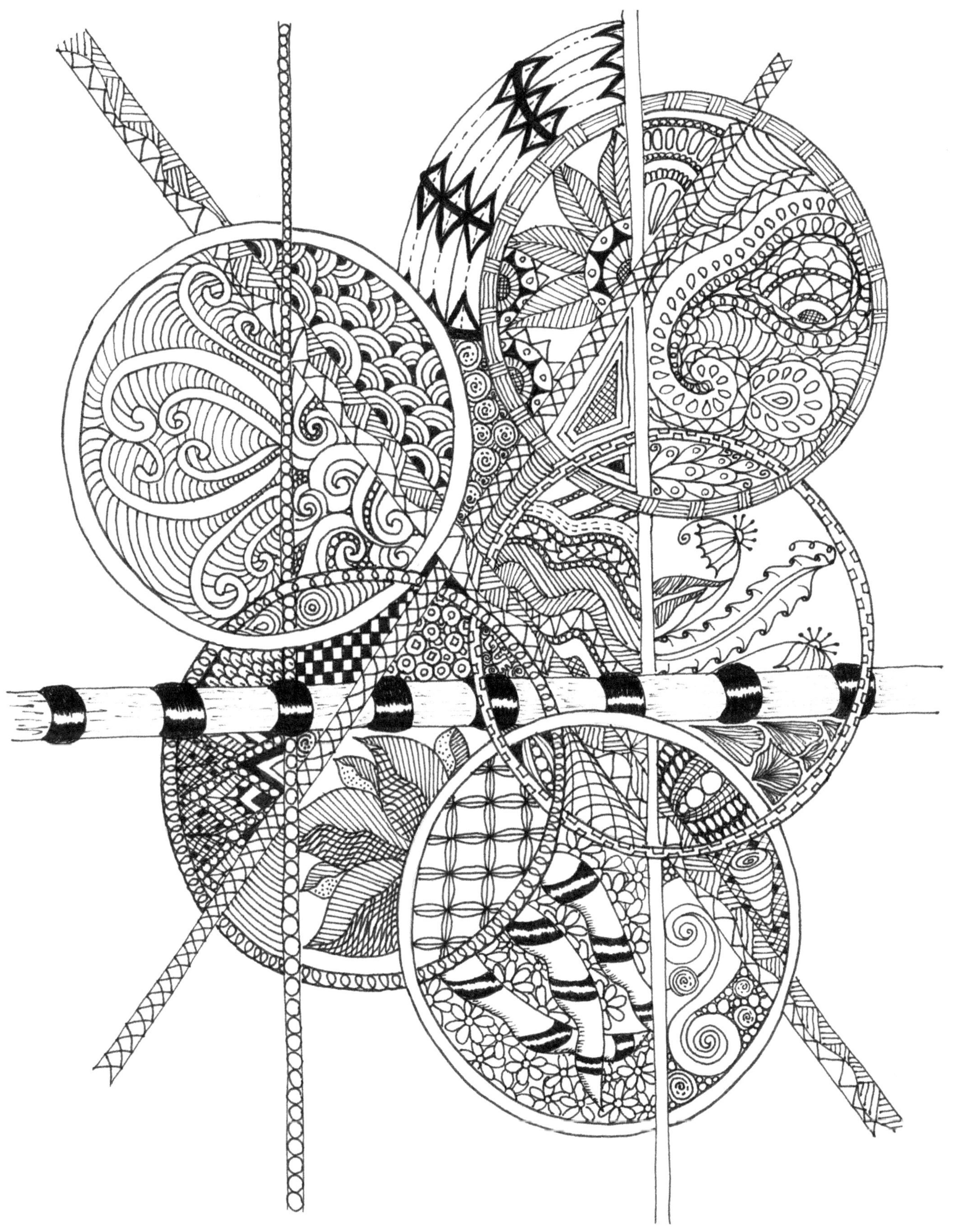

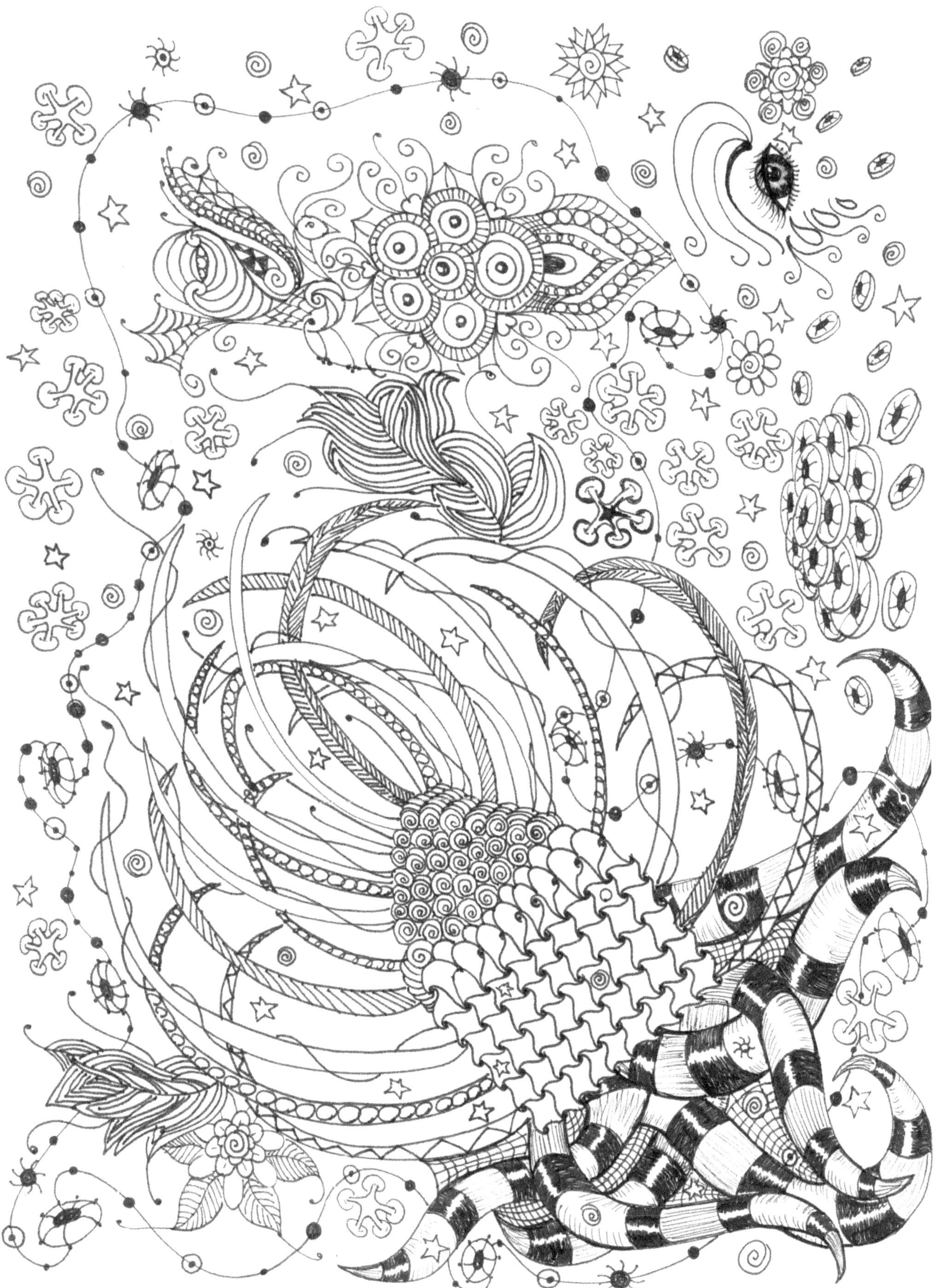

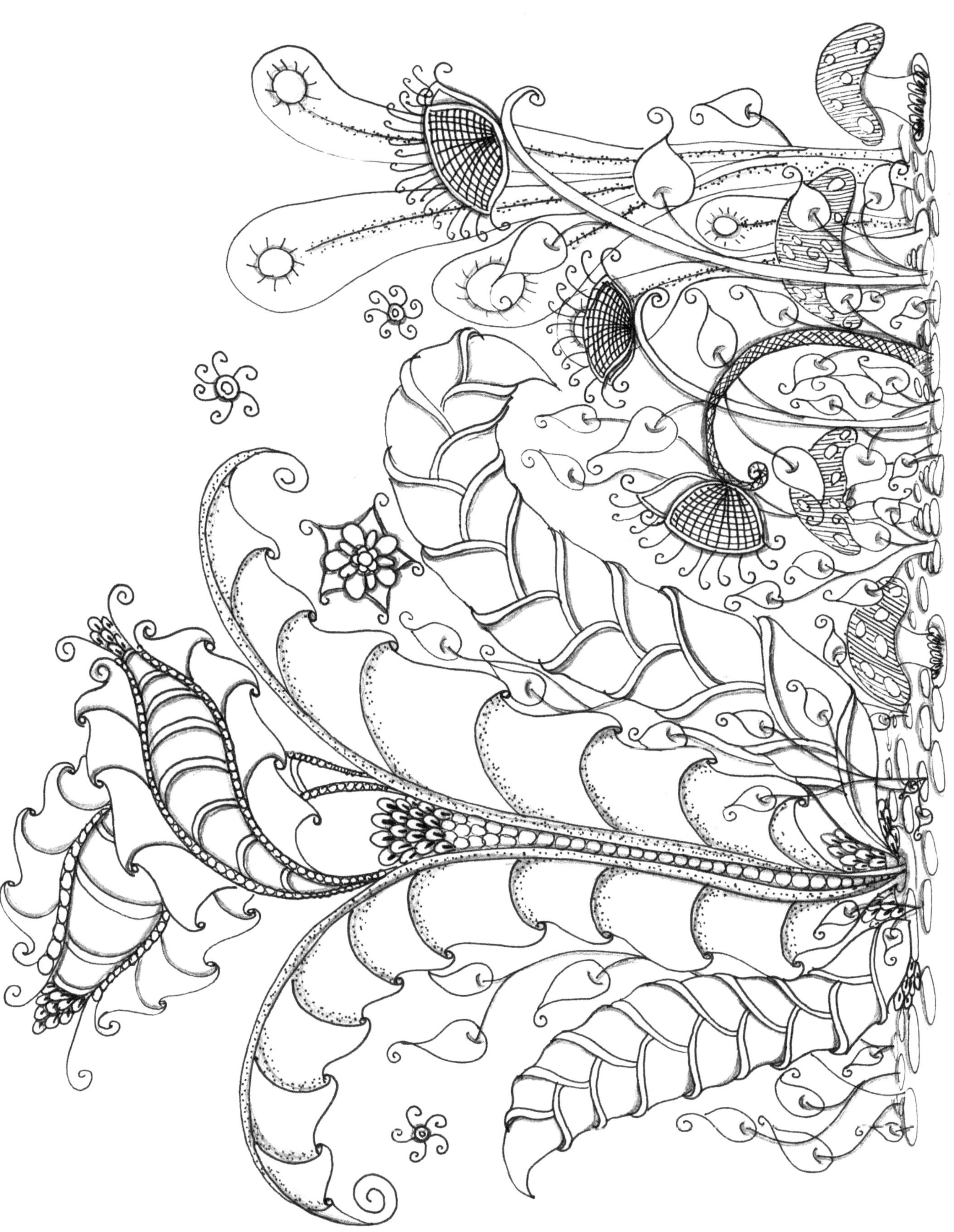

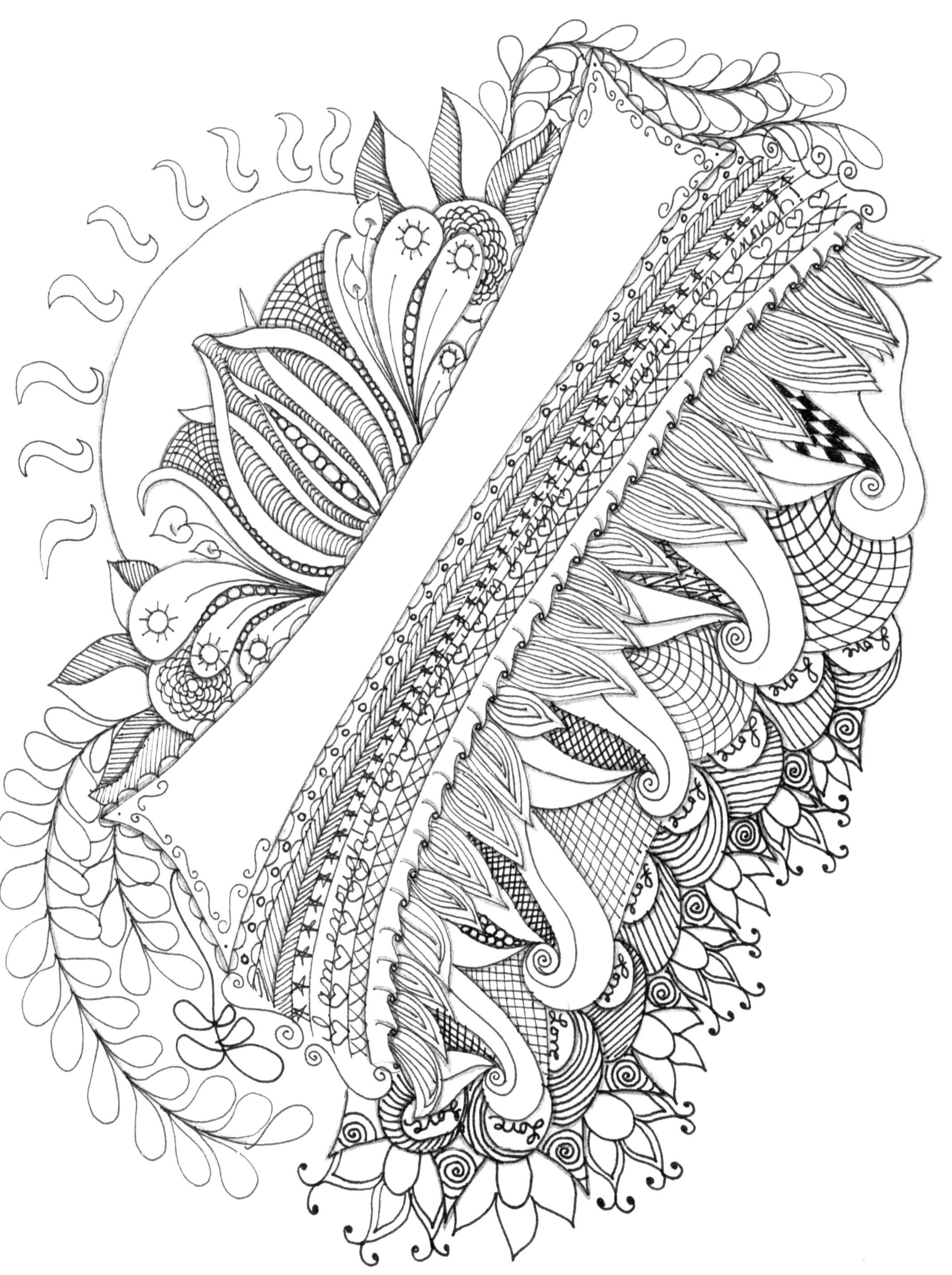

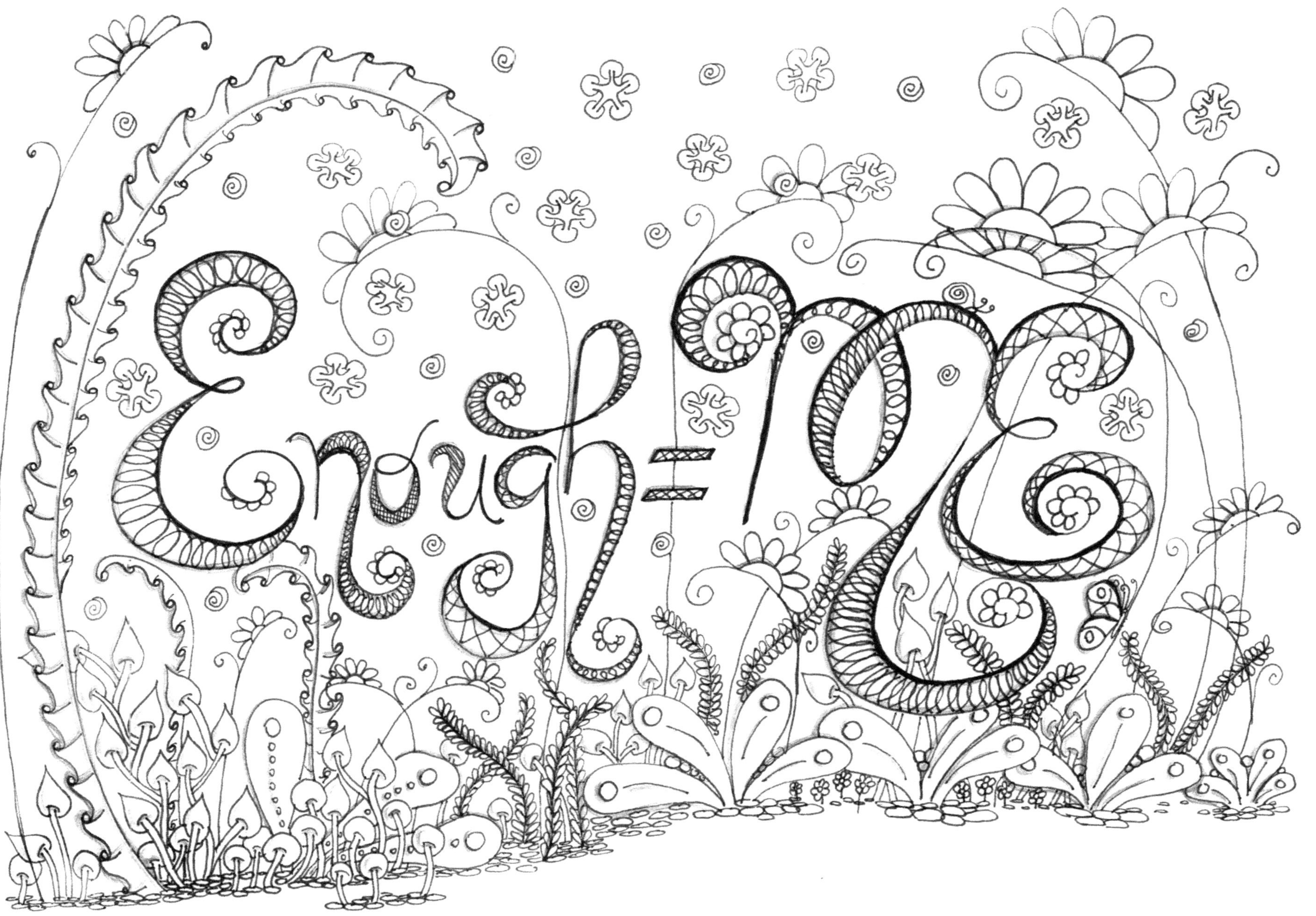
Enough = Me

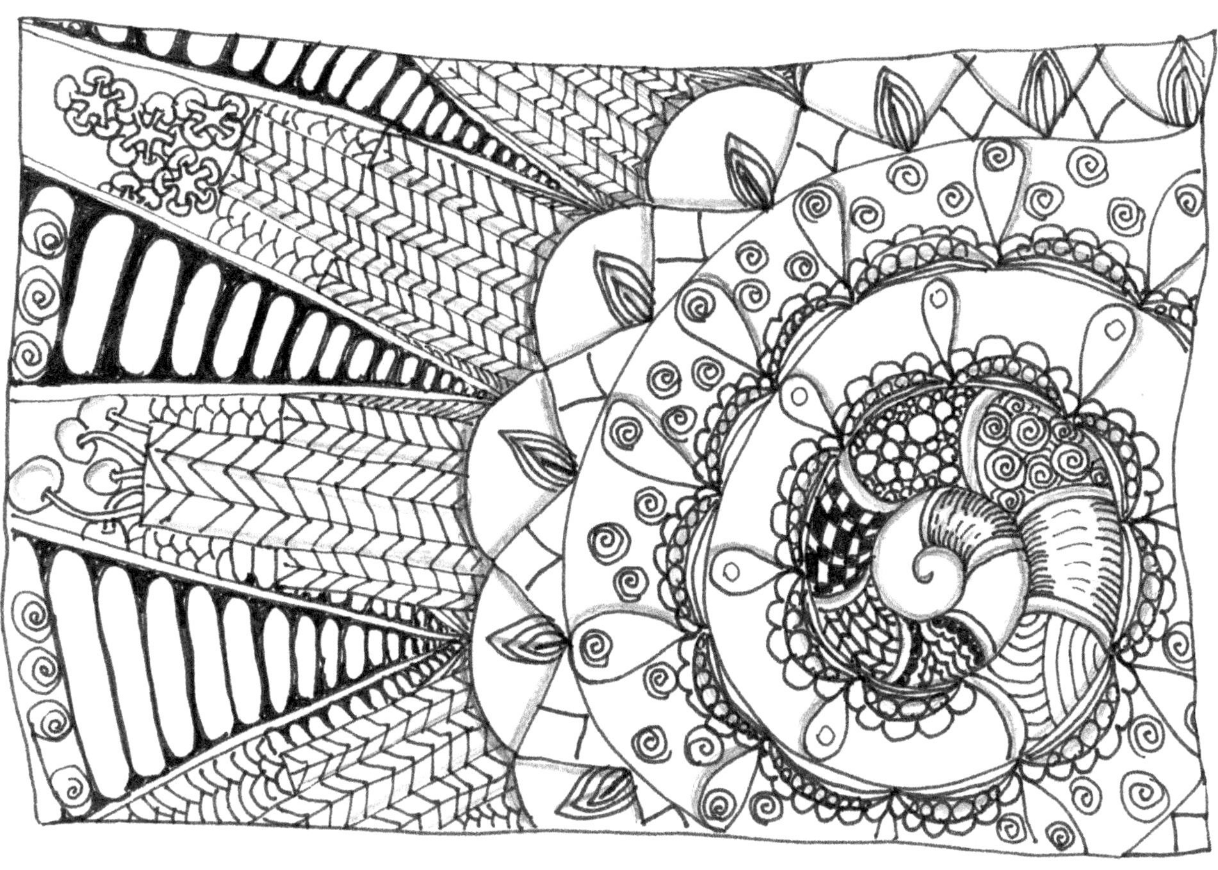

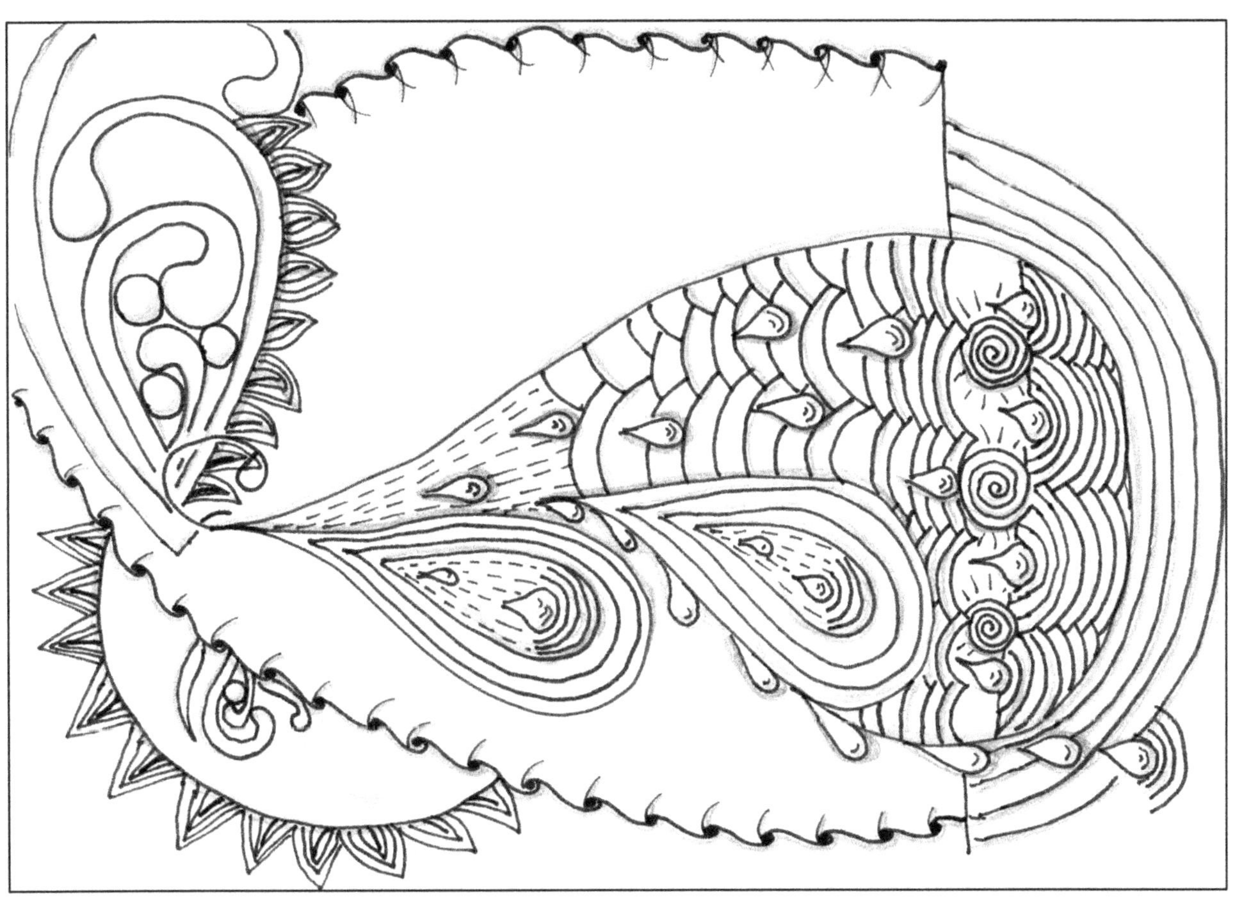

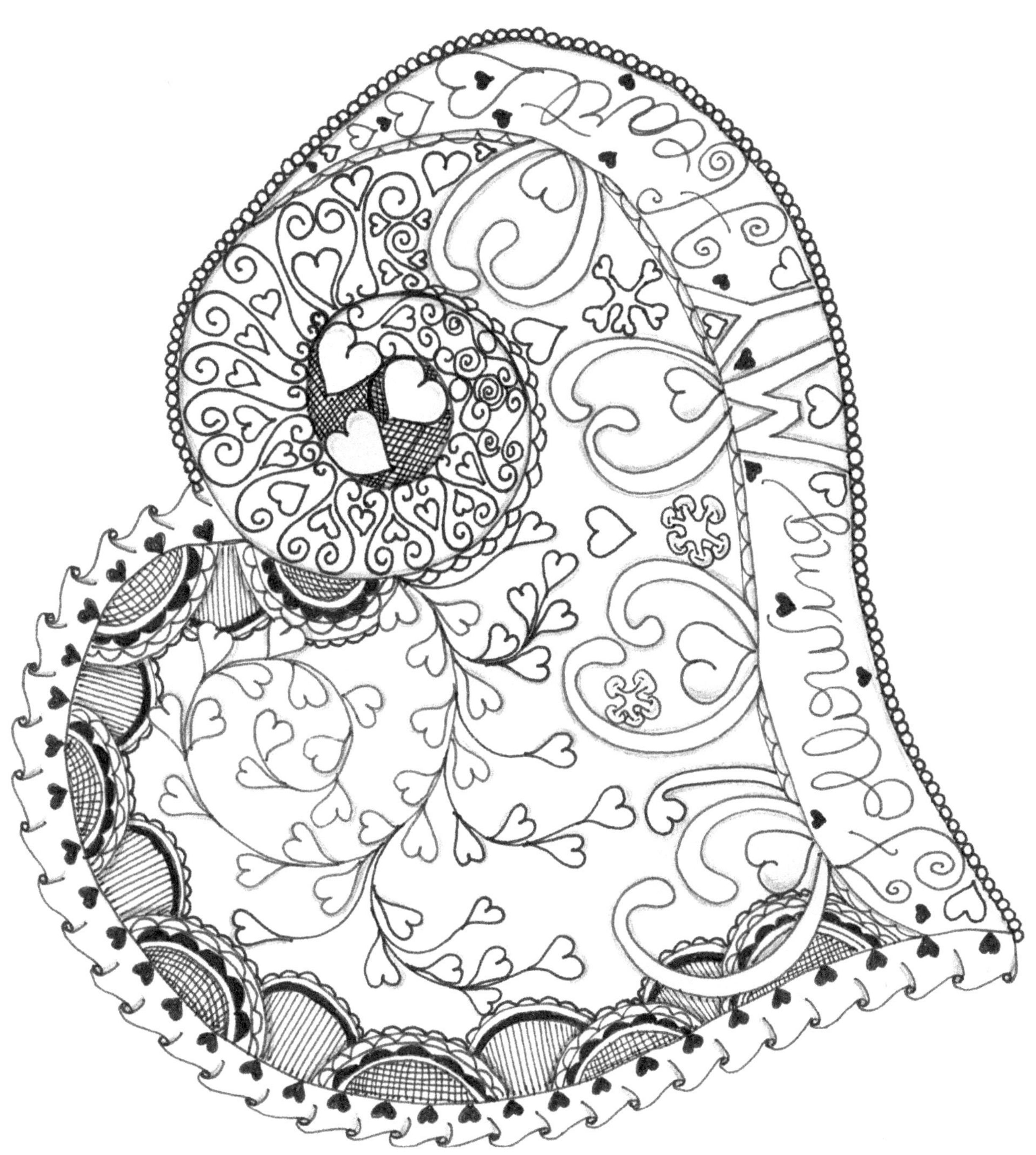

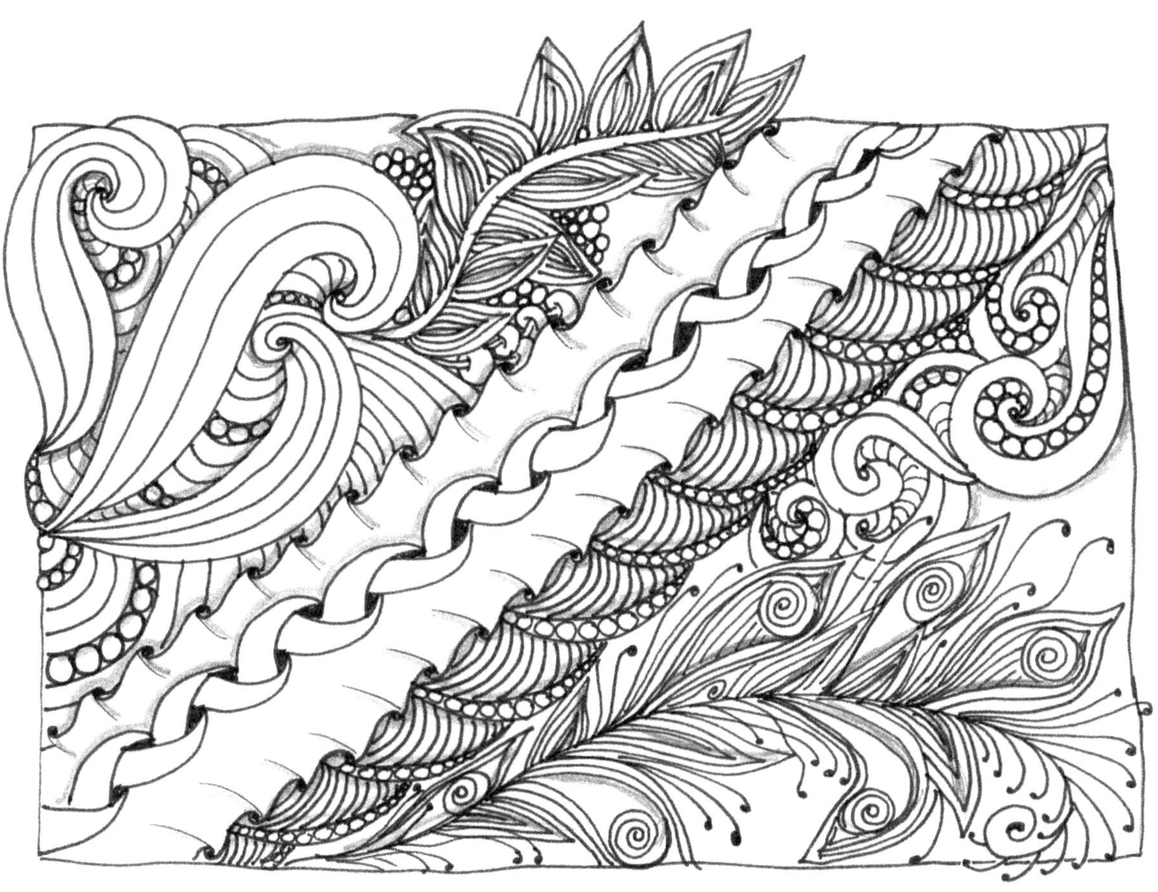

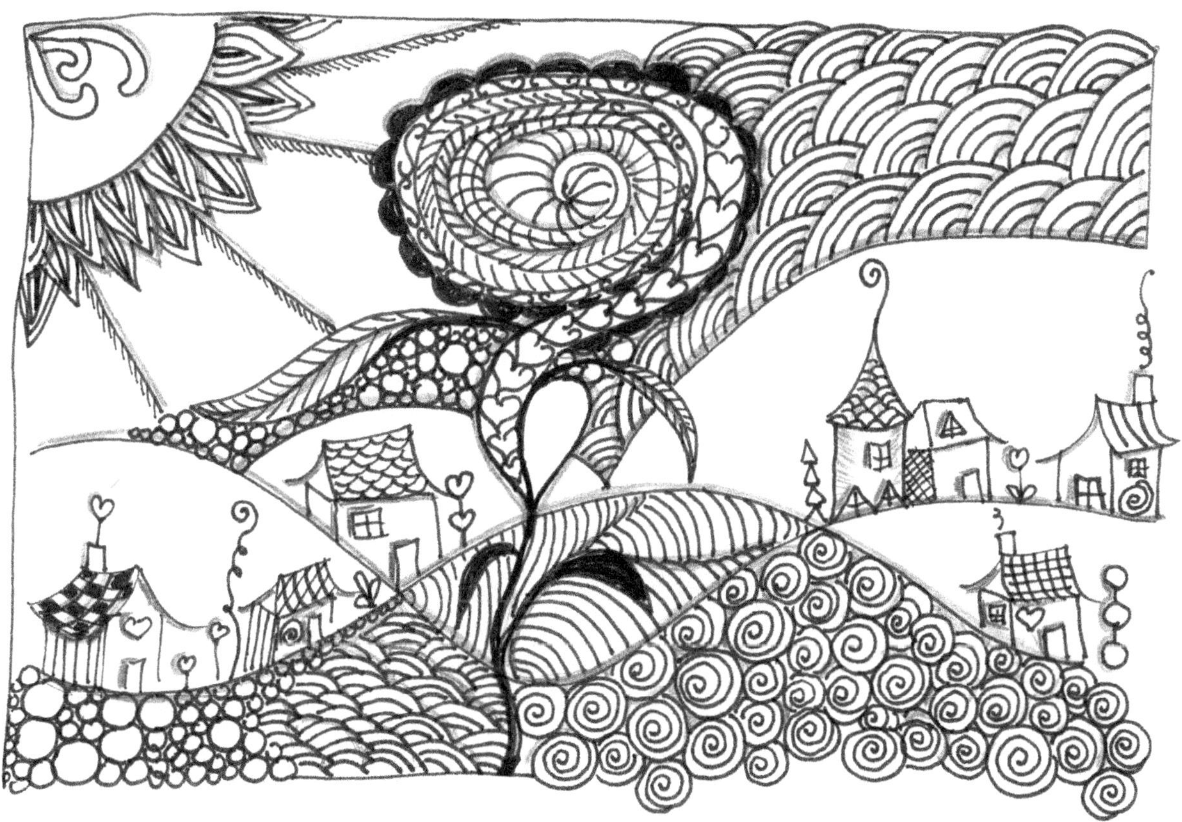

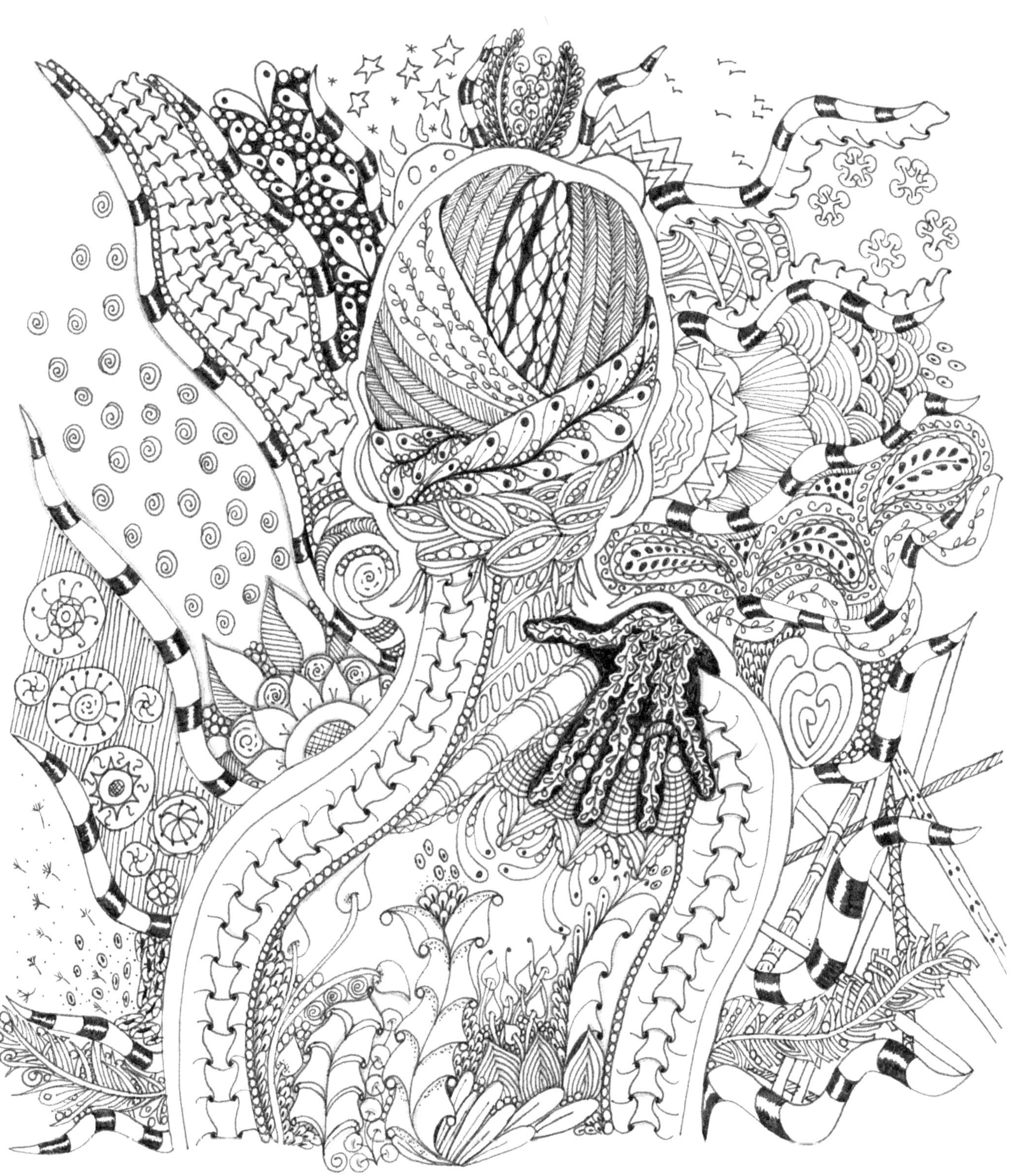

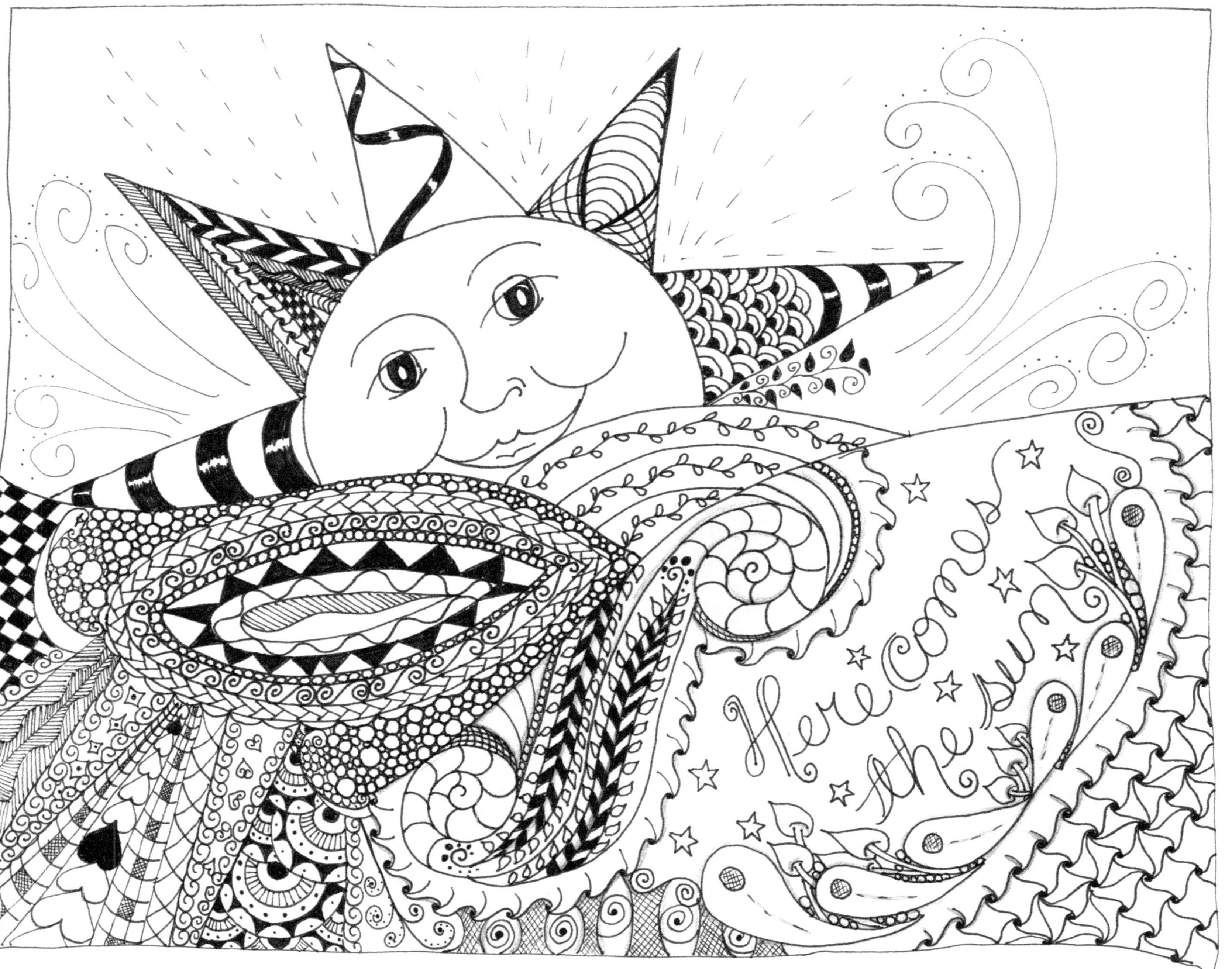
Here comes
the sun

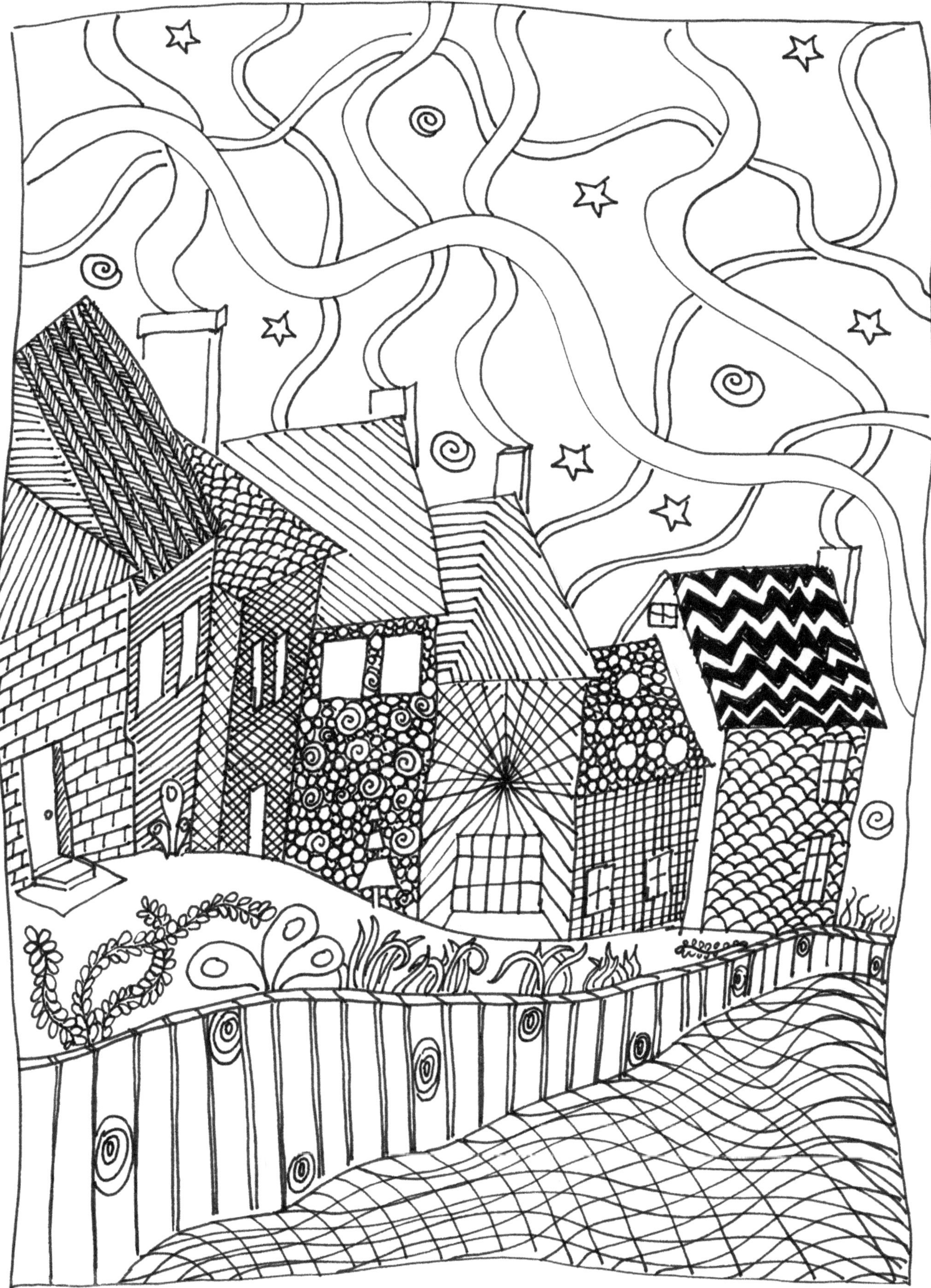

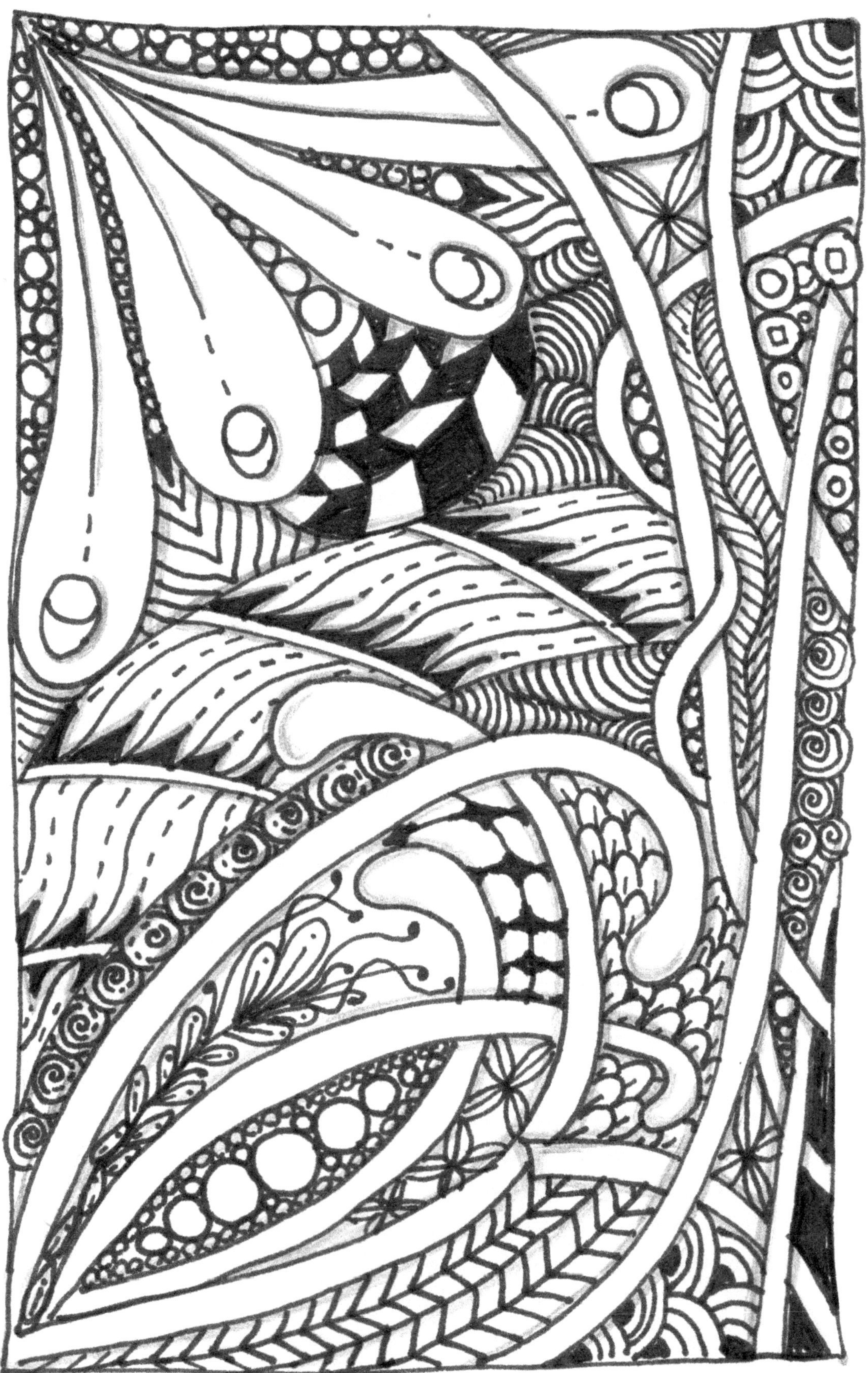

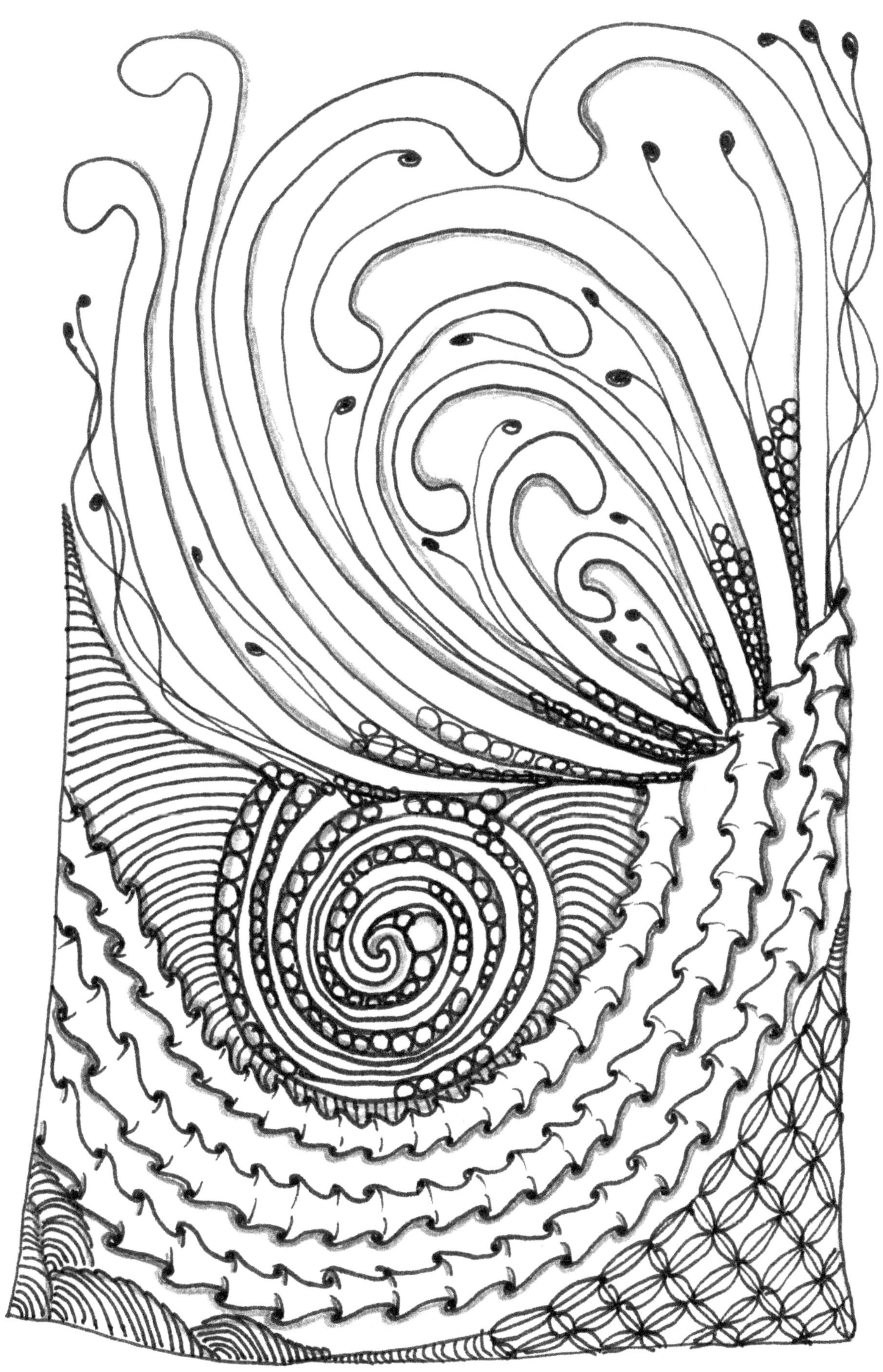

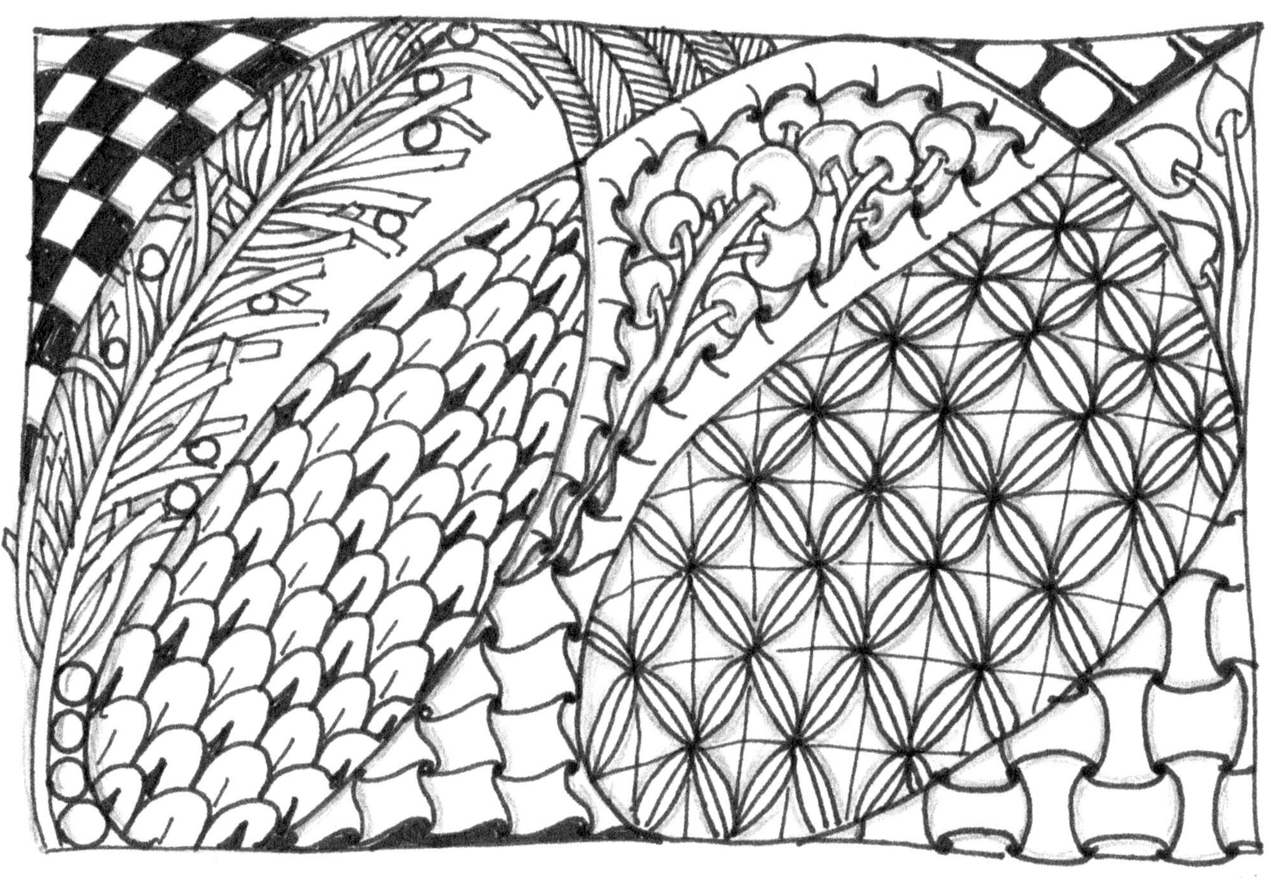

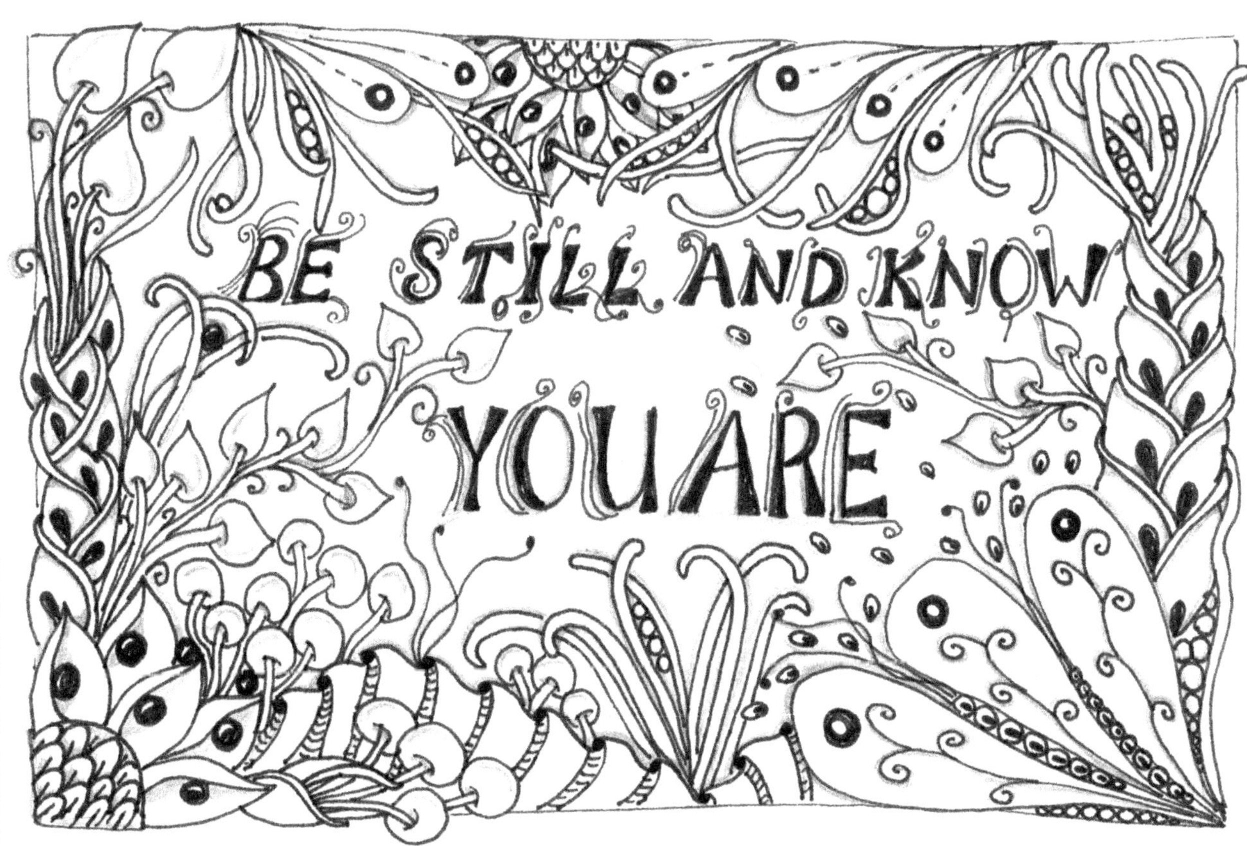
BE STILL AND KNOW
YOU ARE

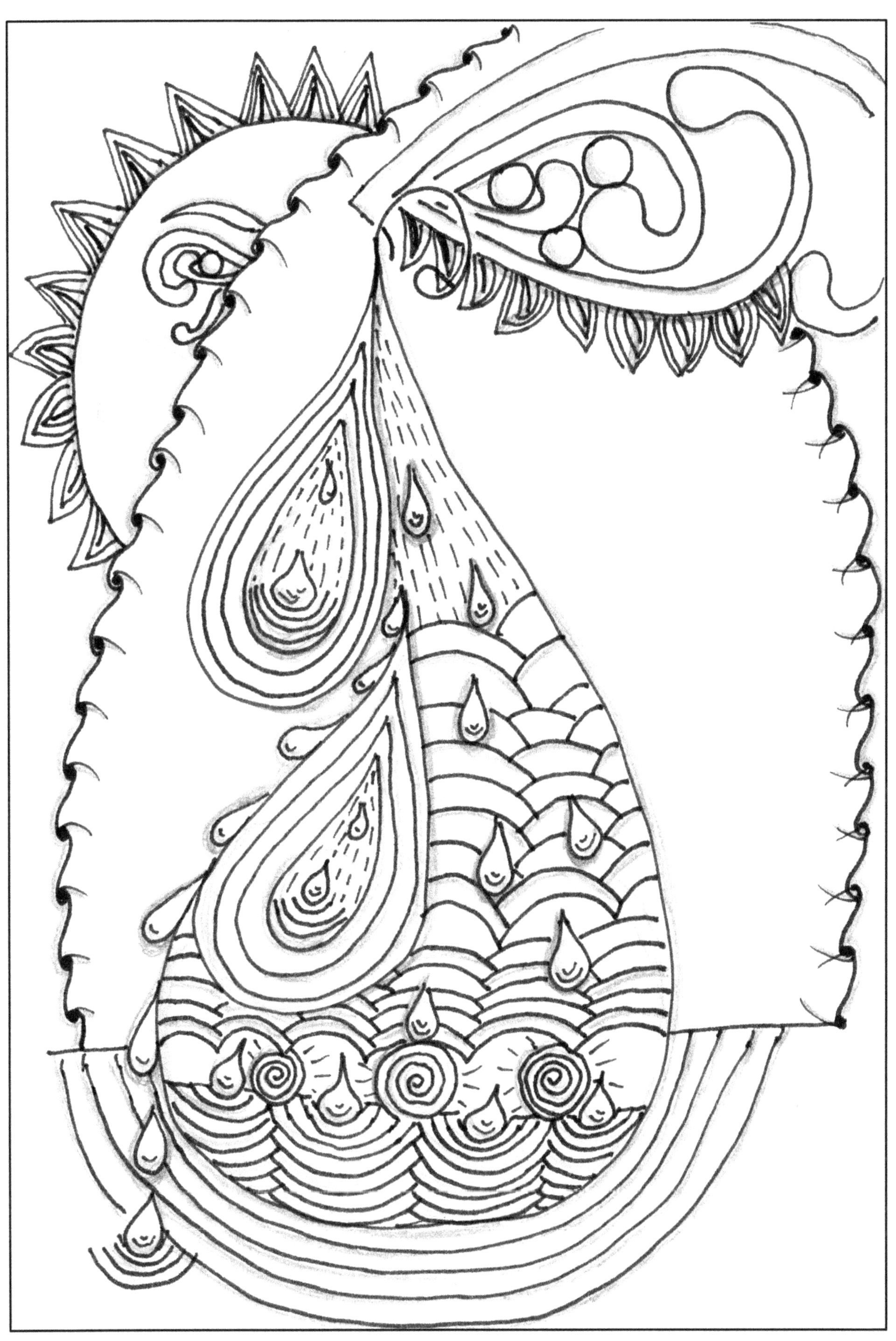

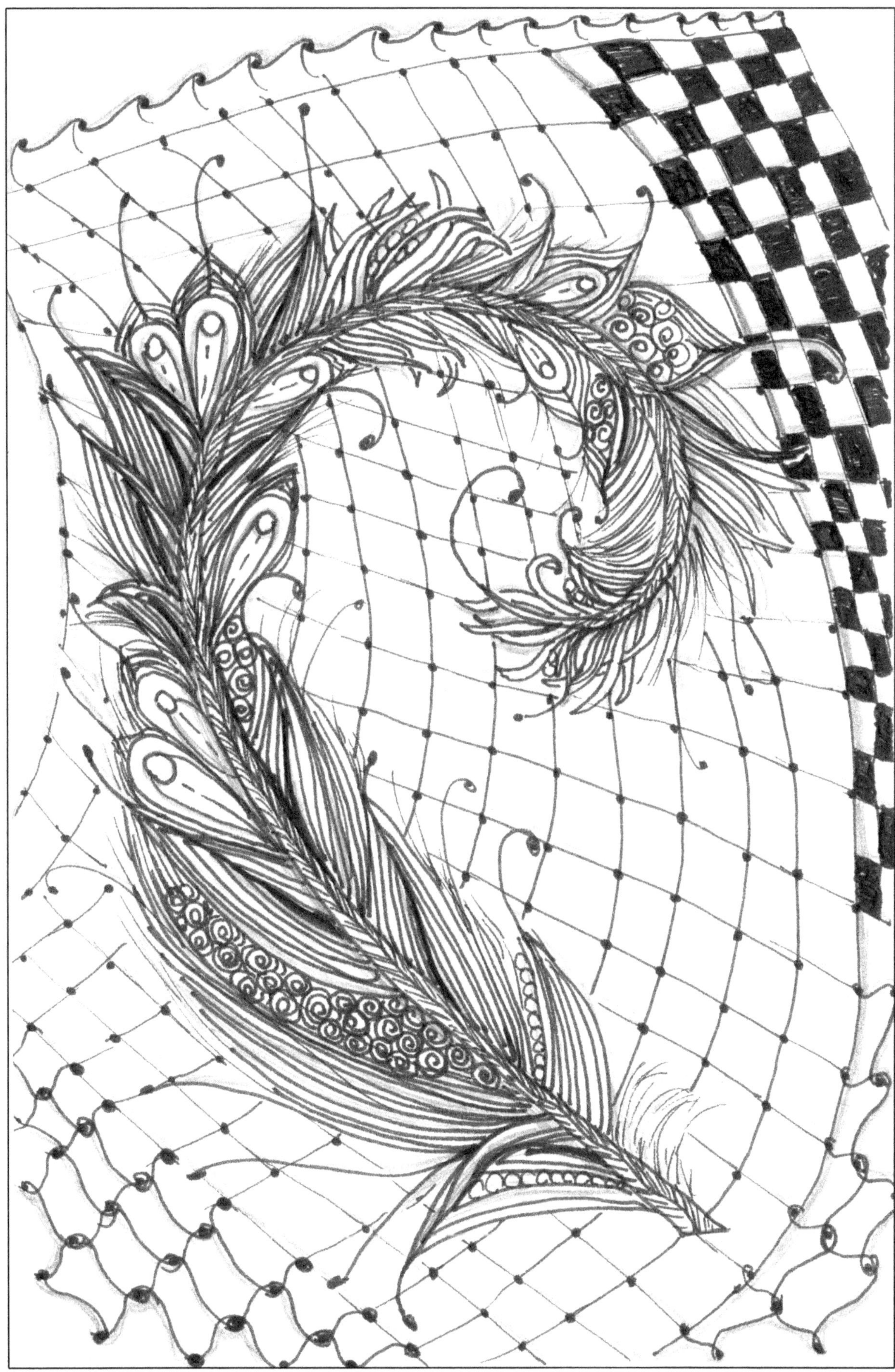

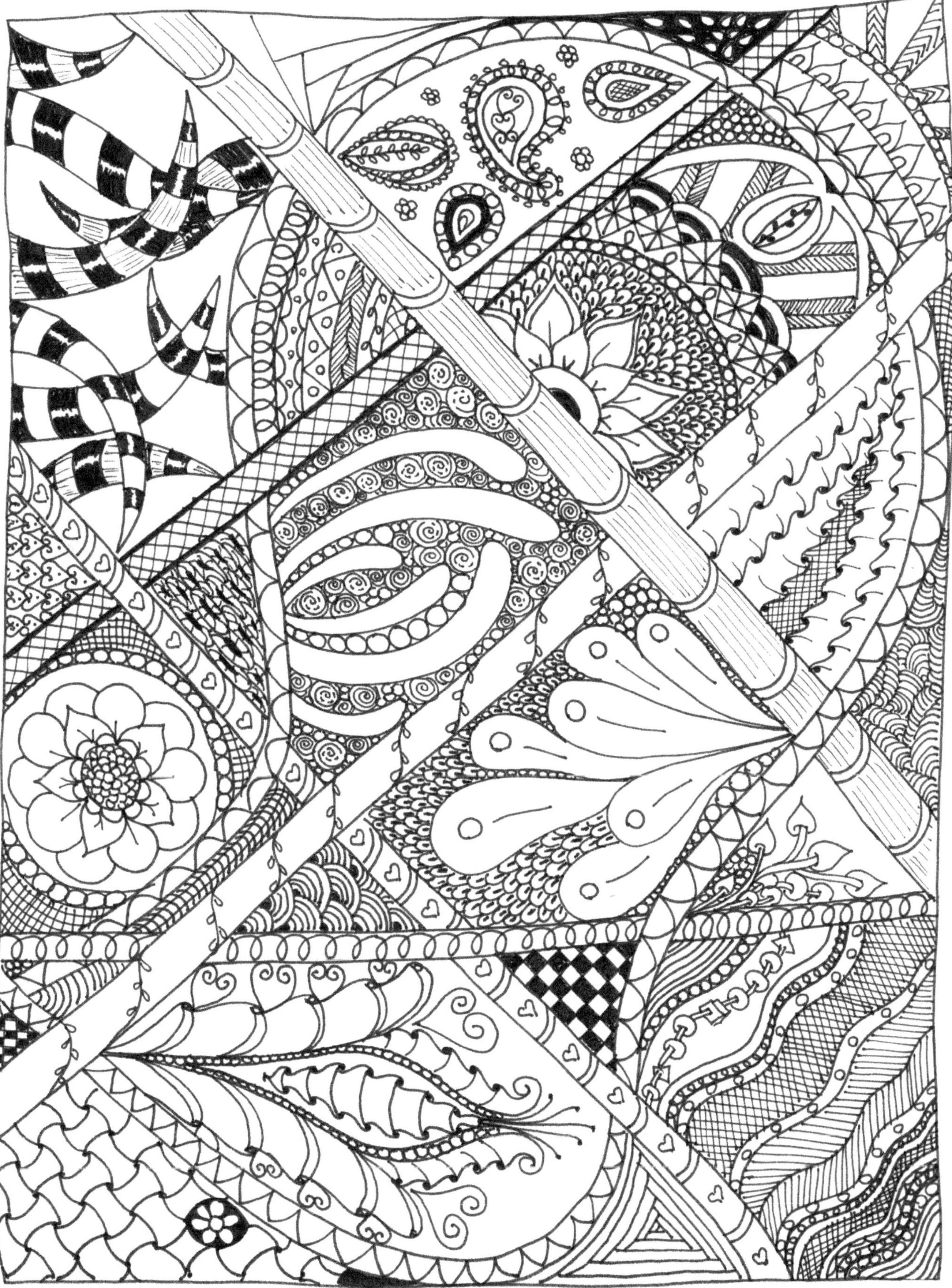

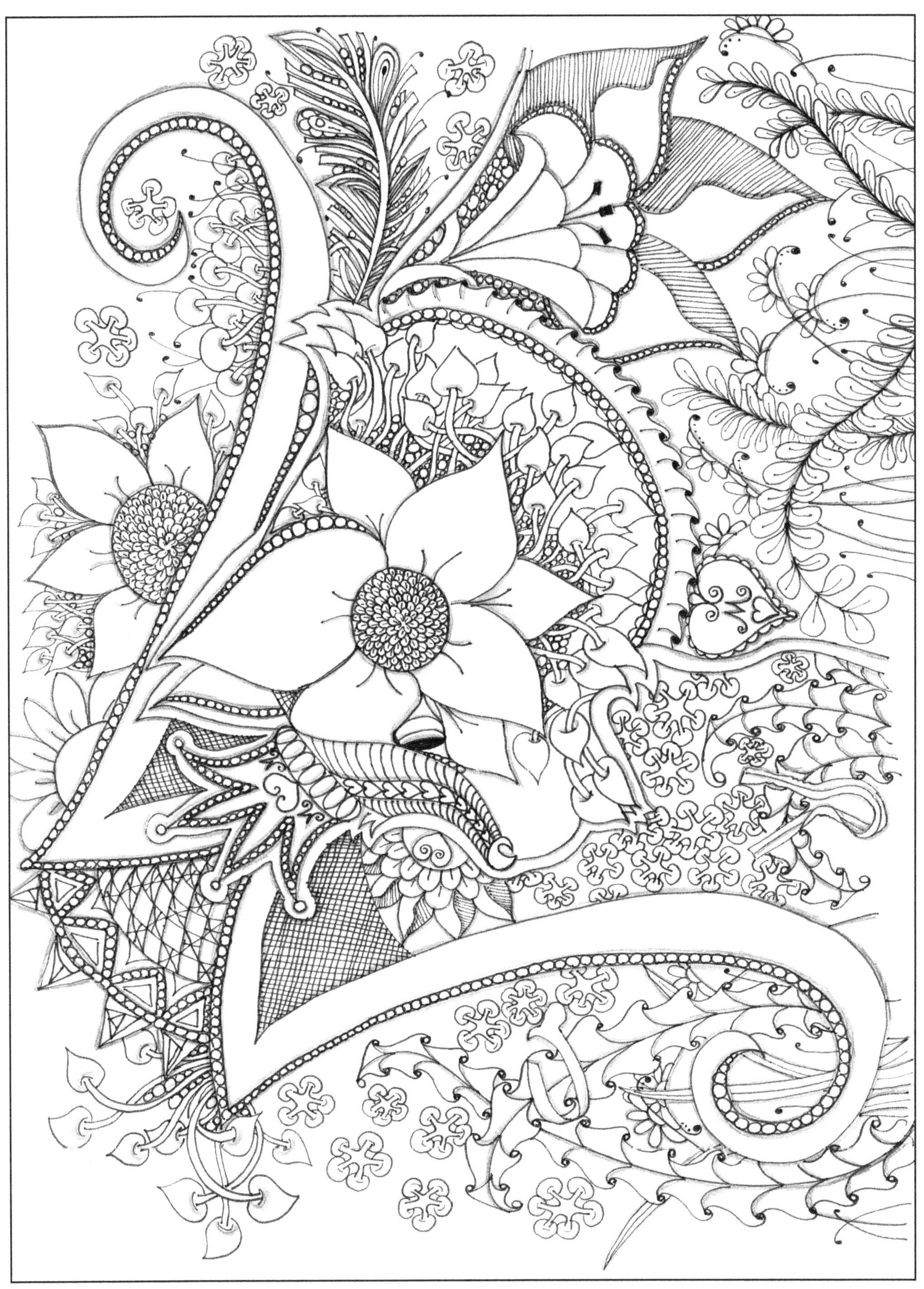

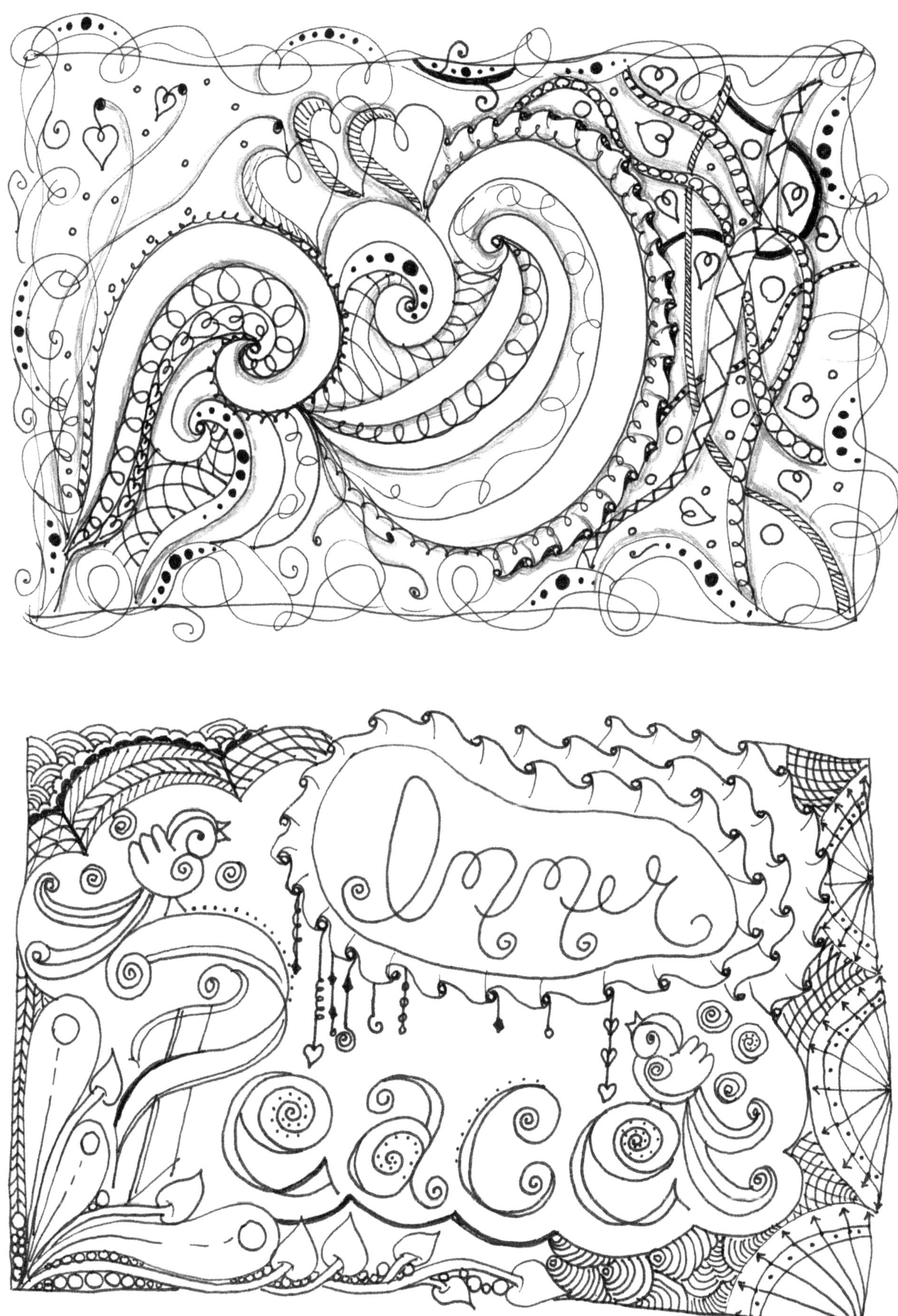
Inner
Peace

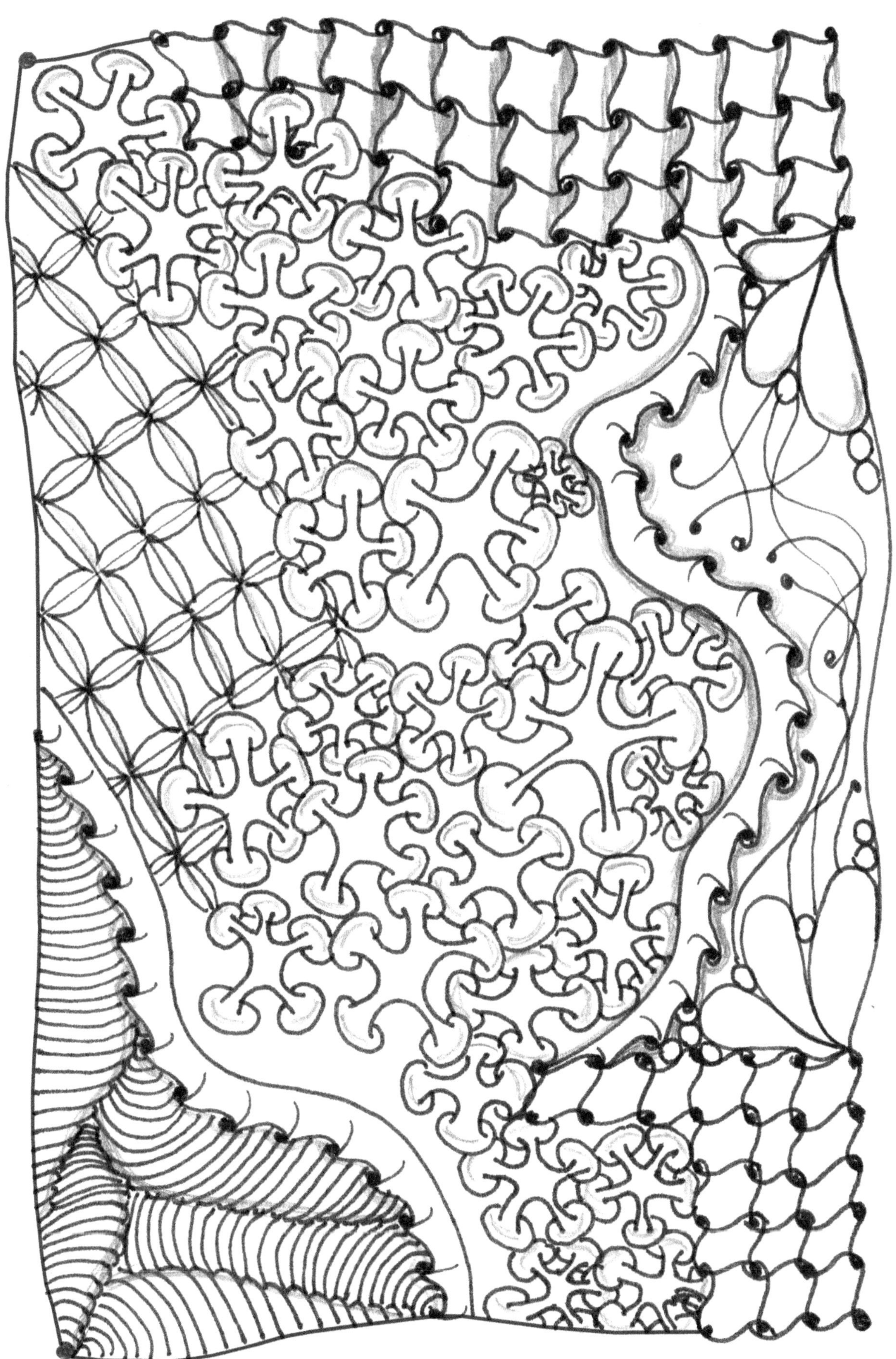

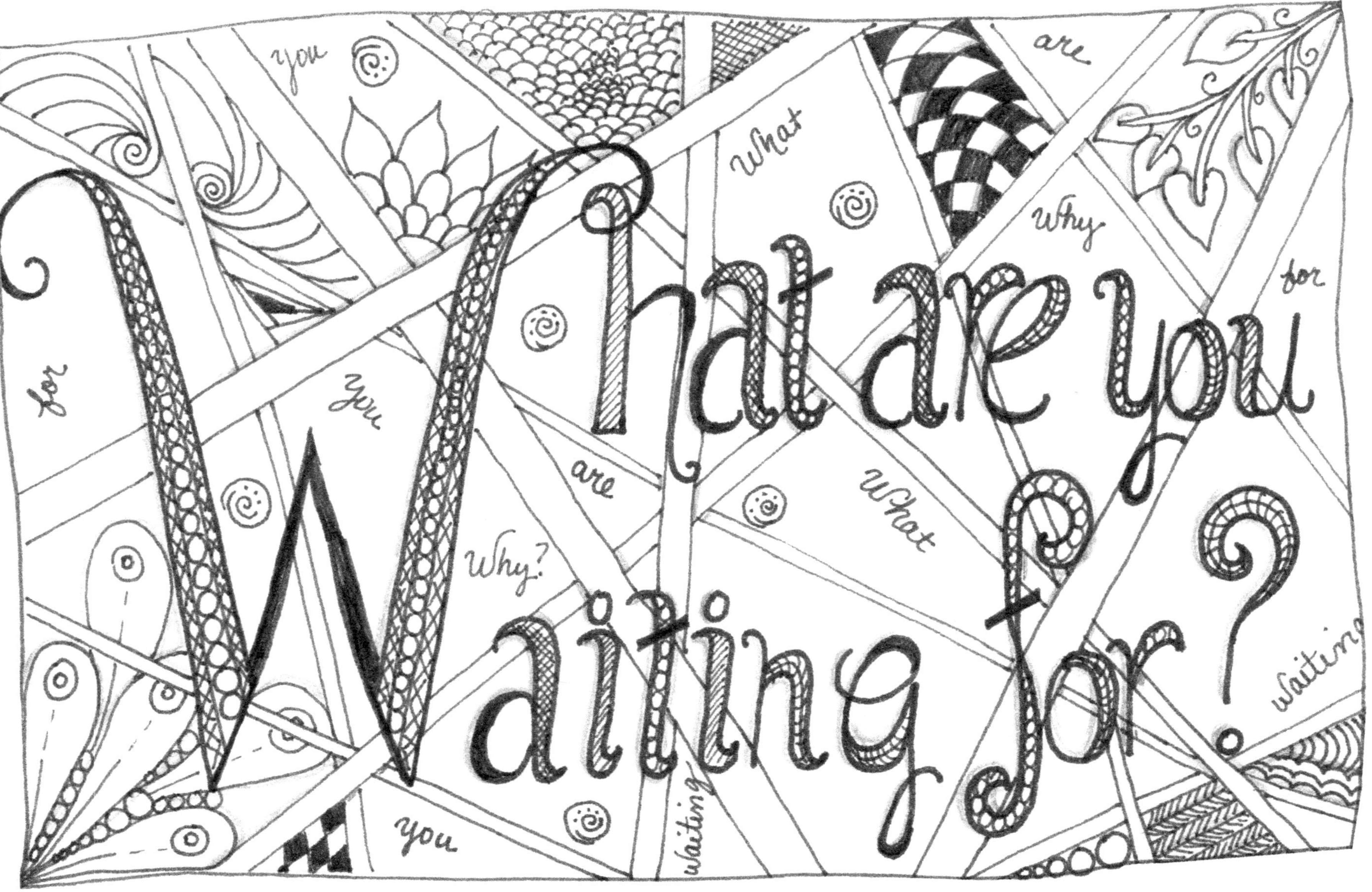
What are you
Waiting for?

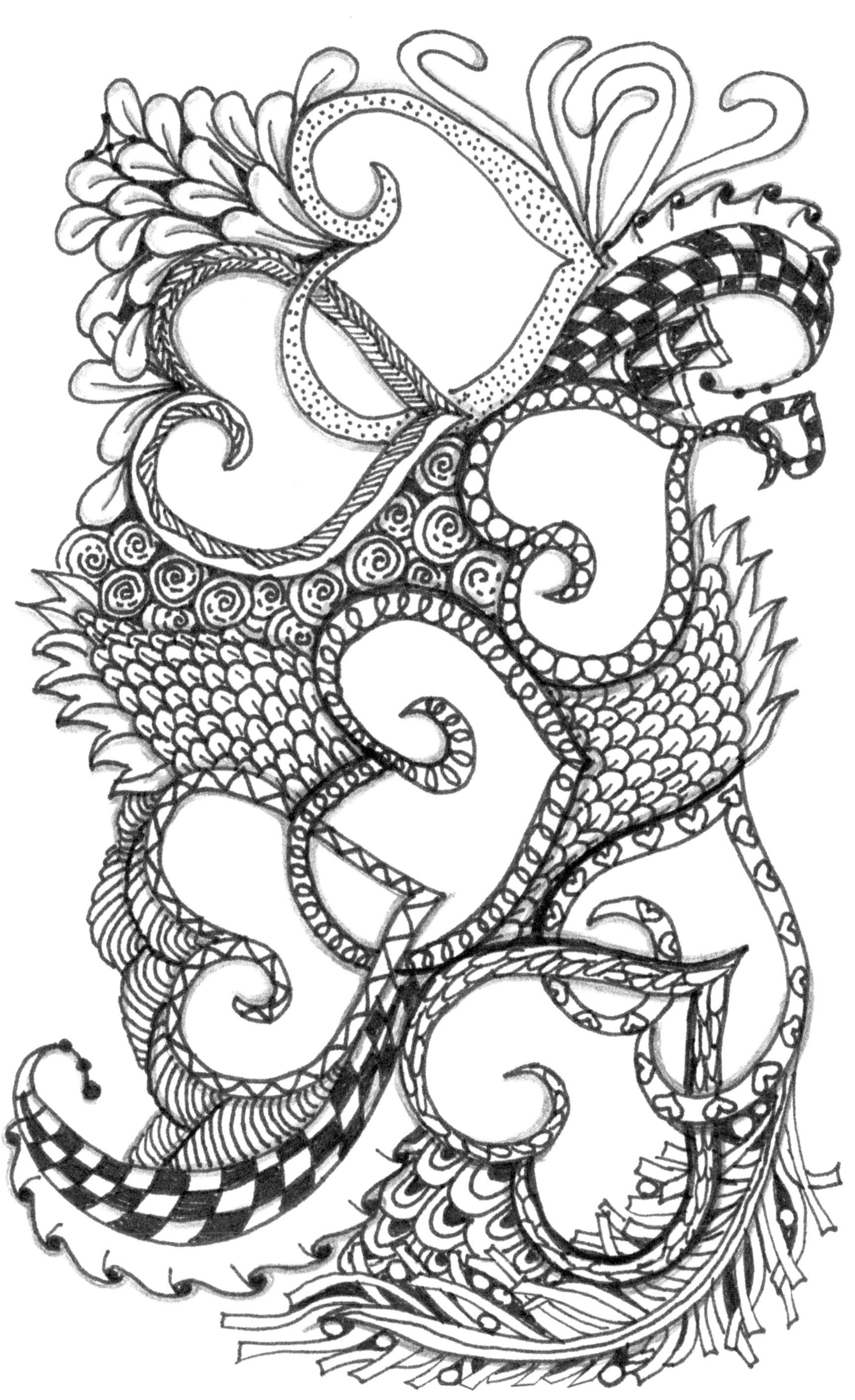

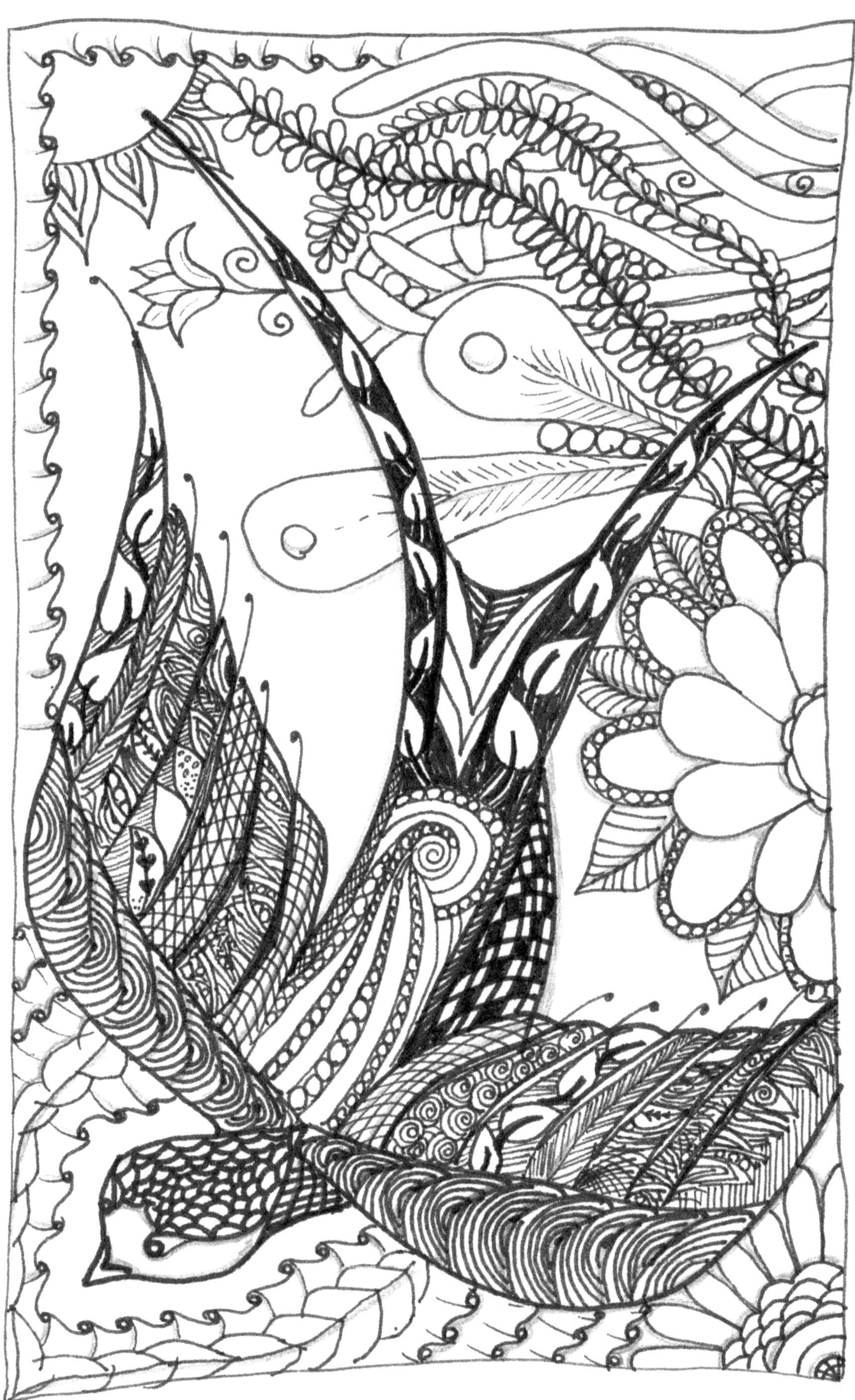

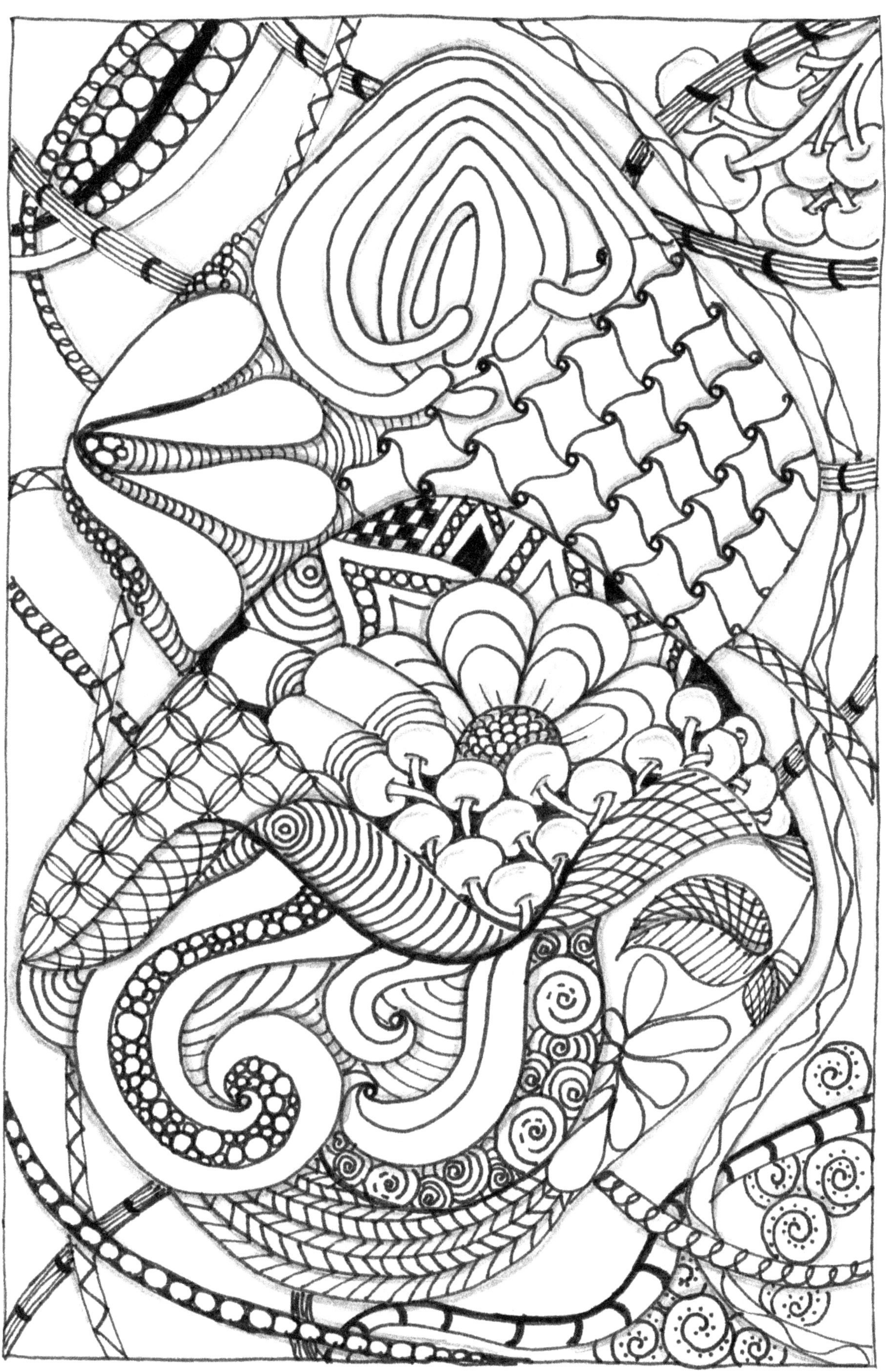

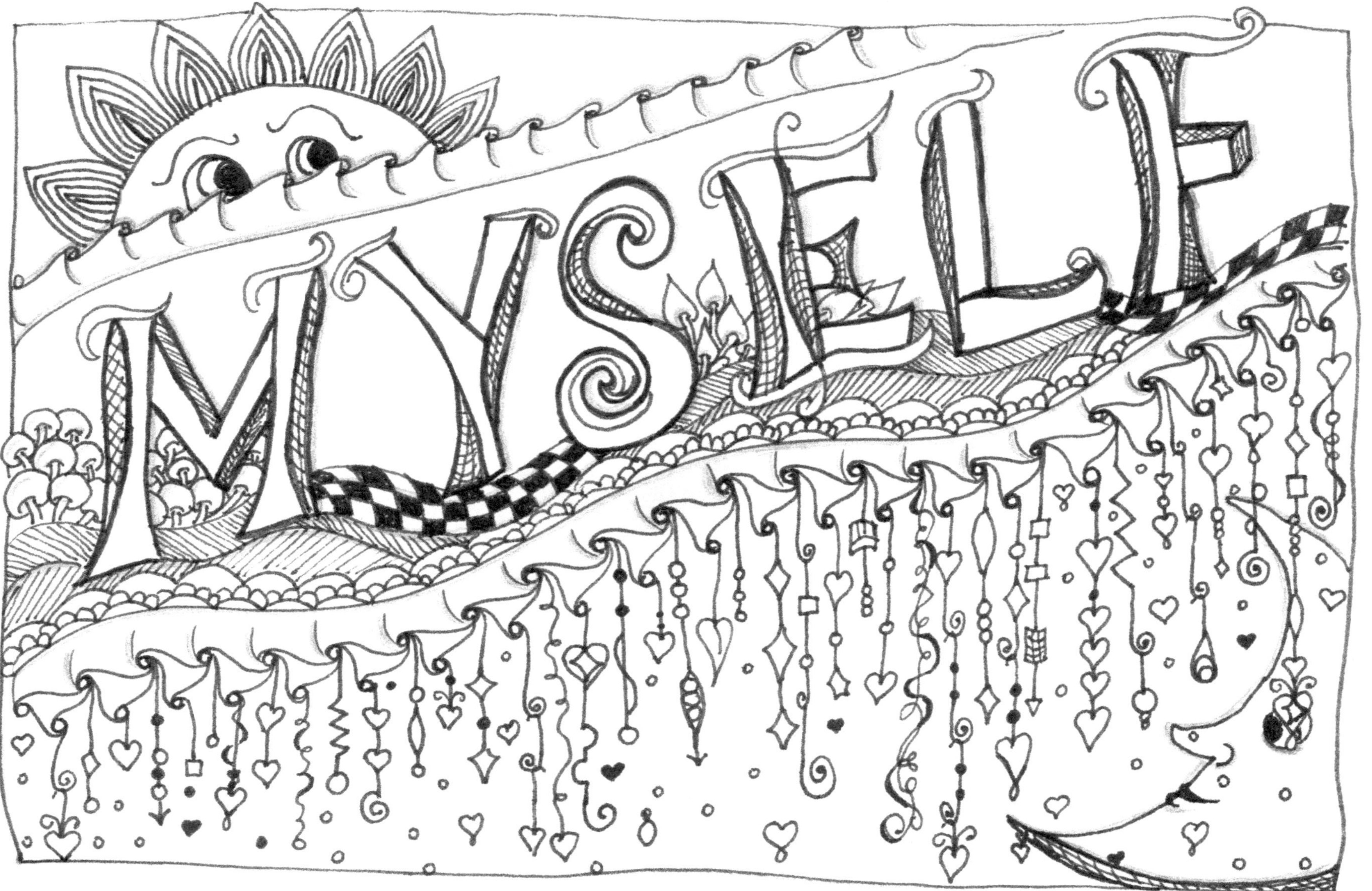
MYSELF

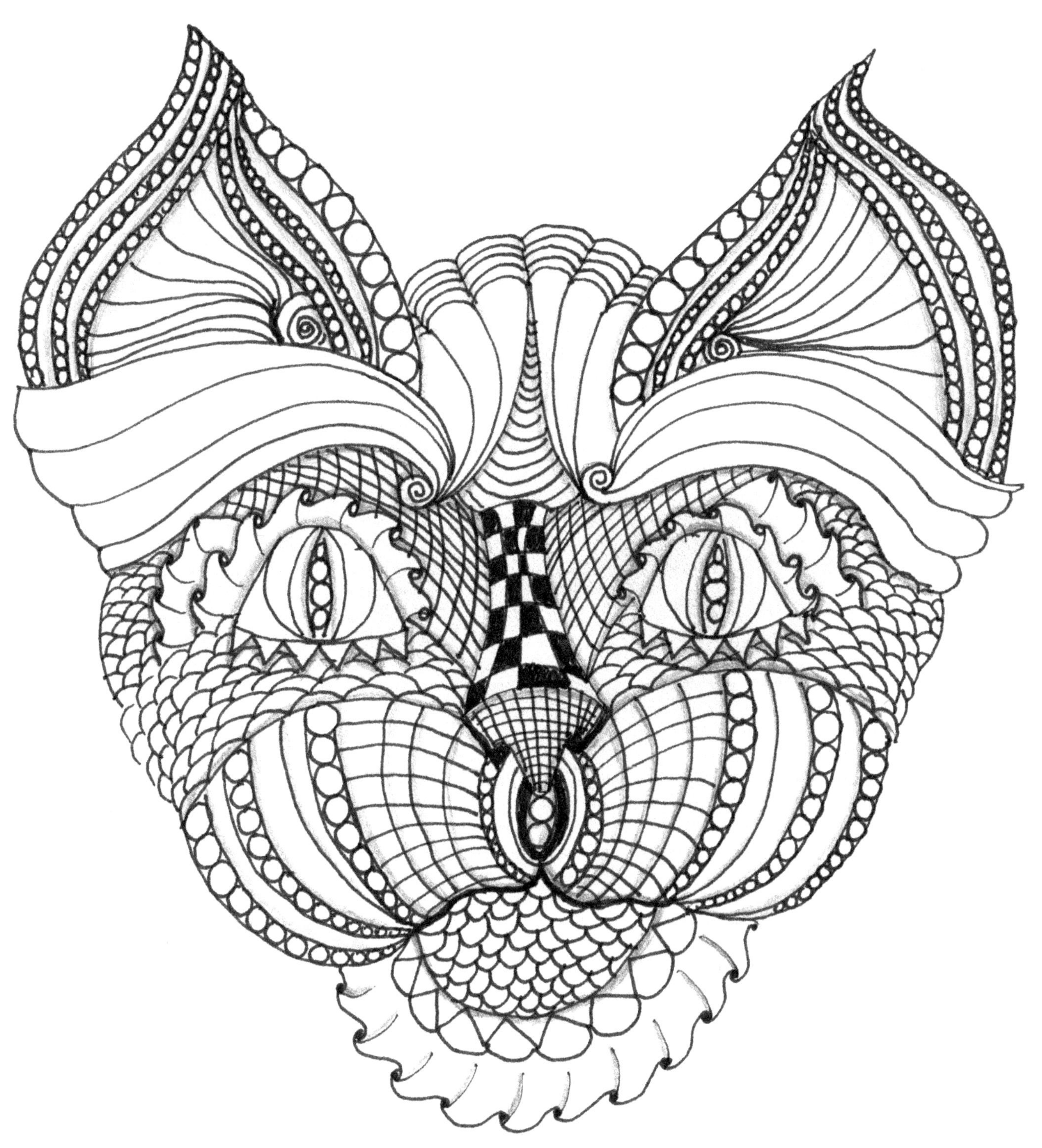

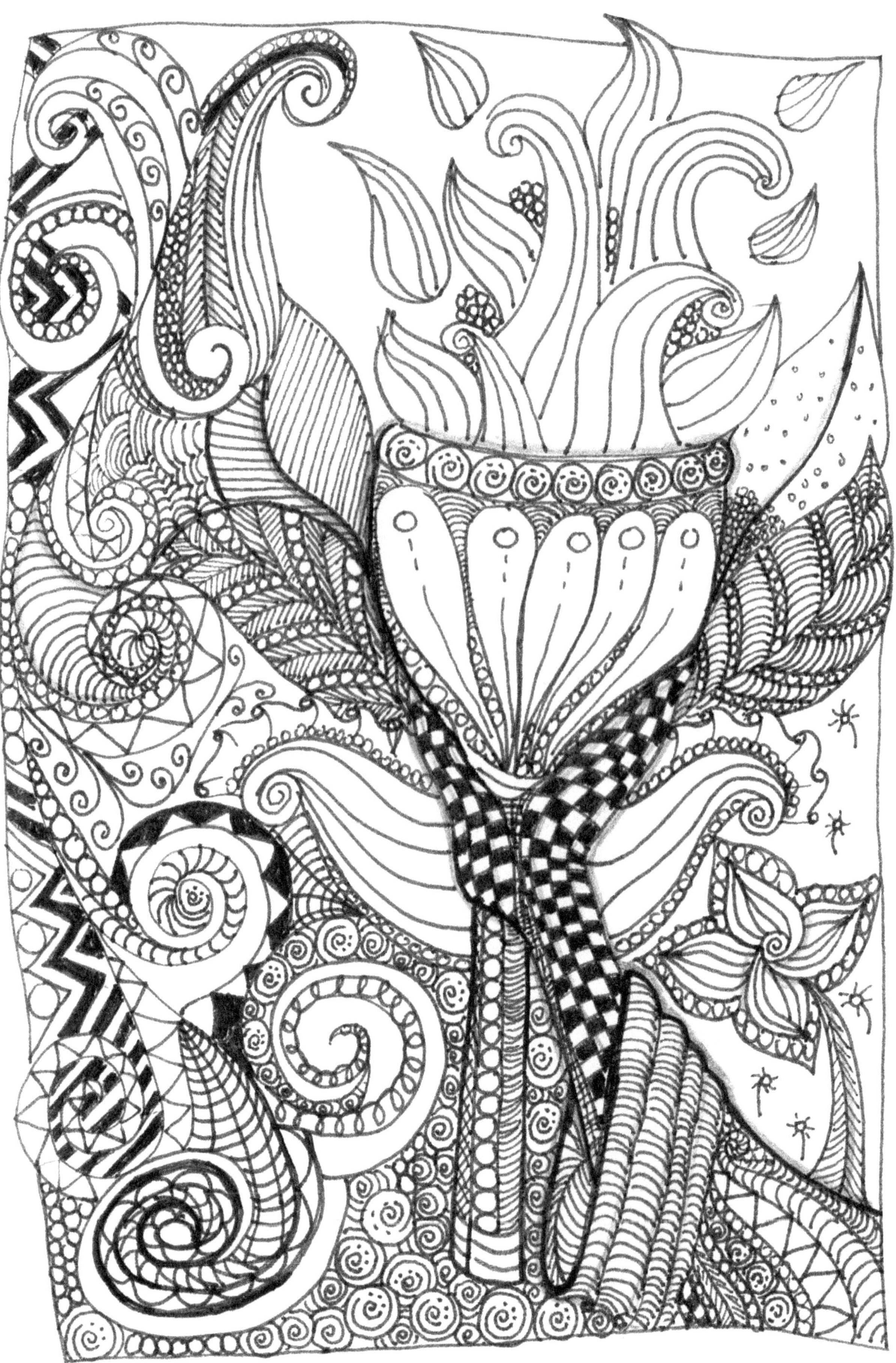

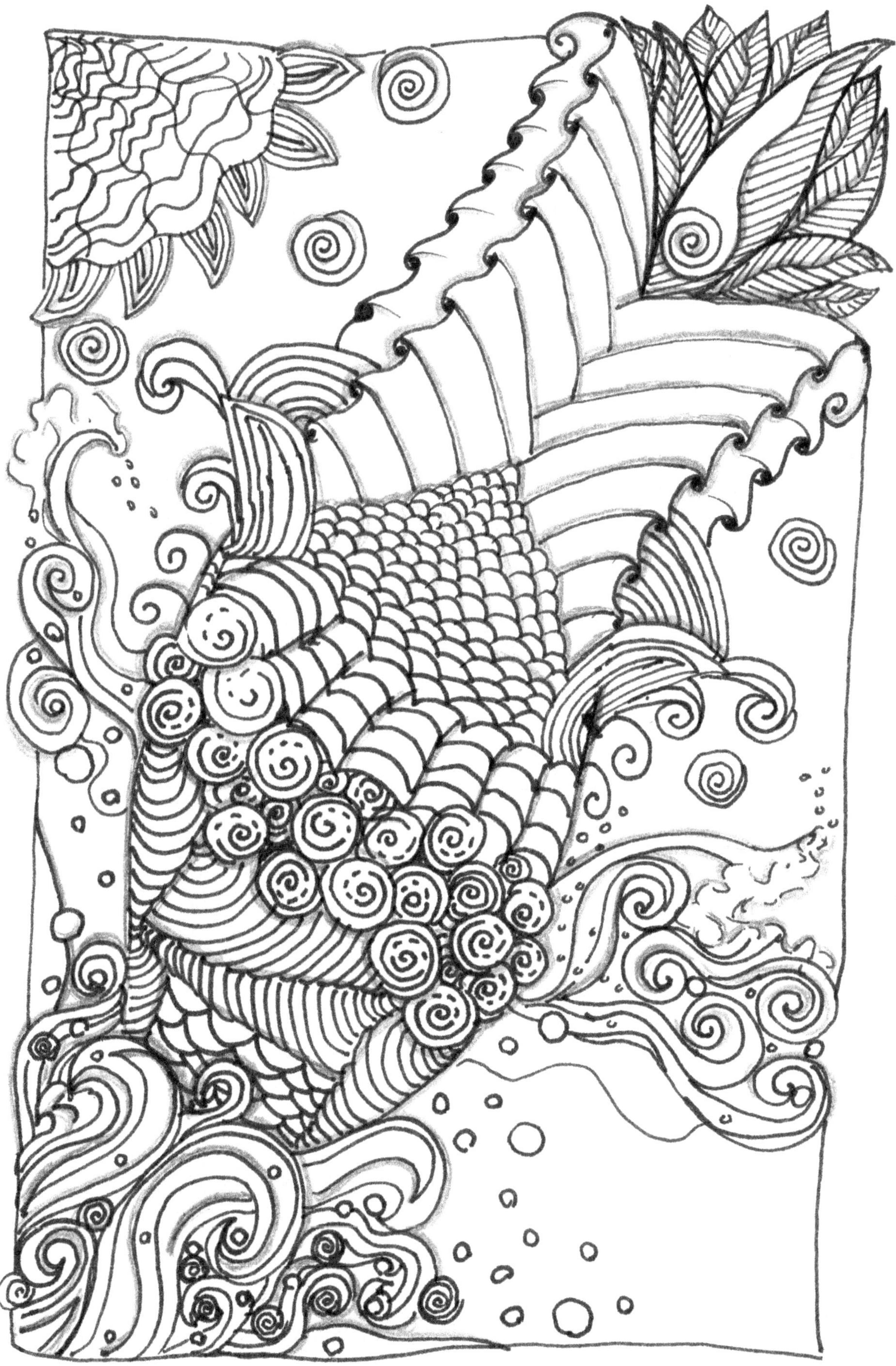

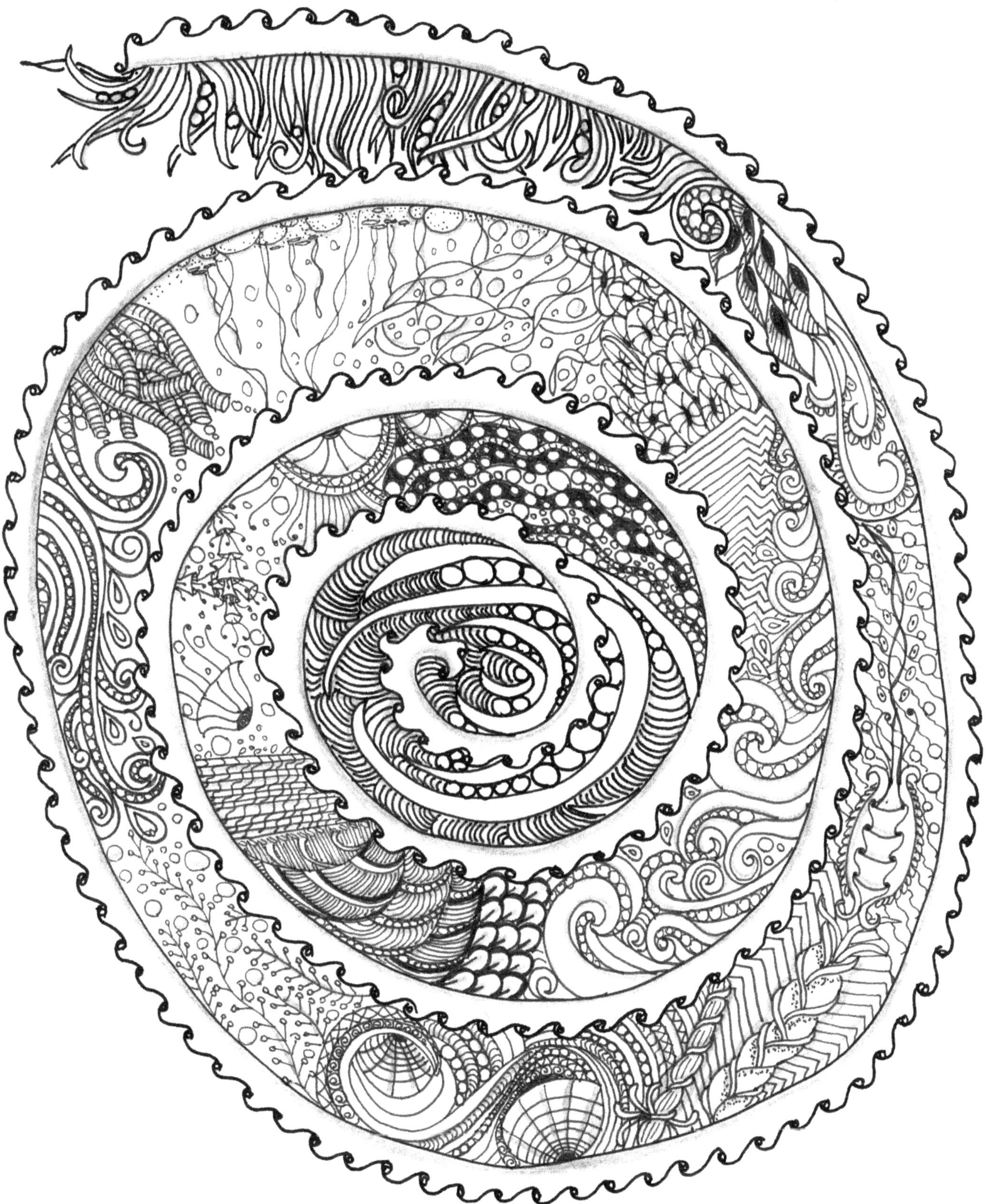

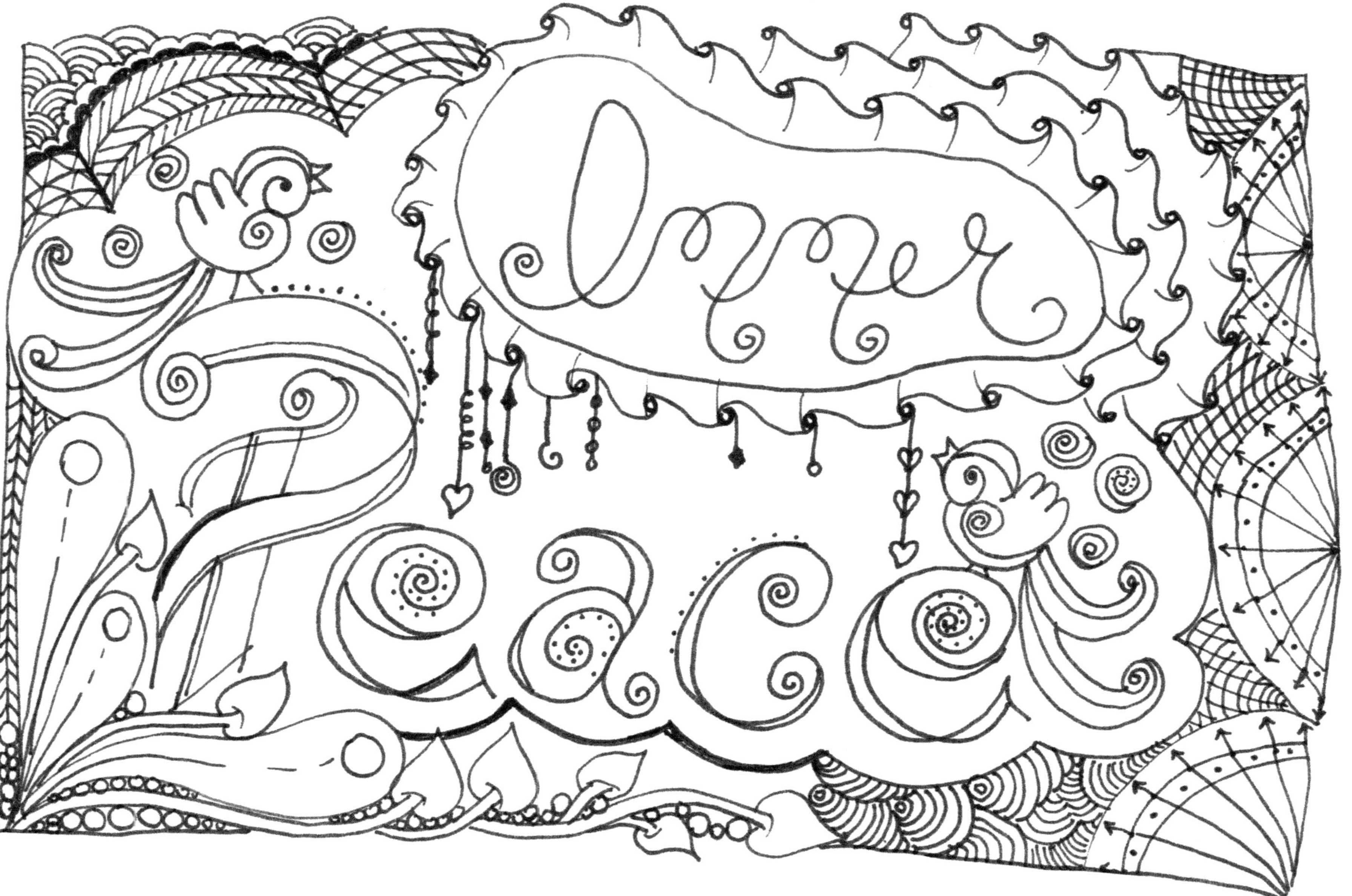
Inner
Peace

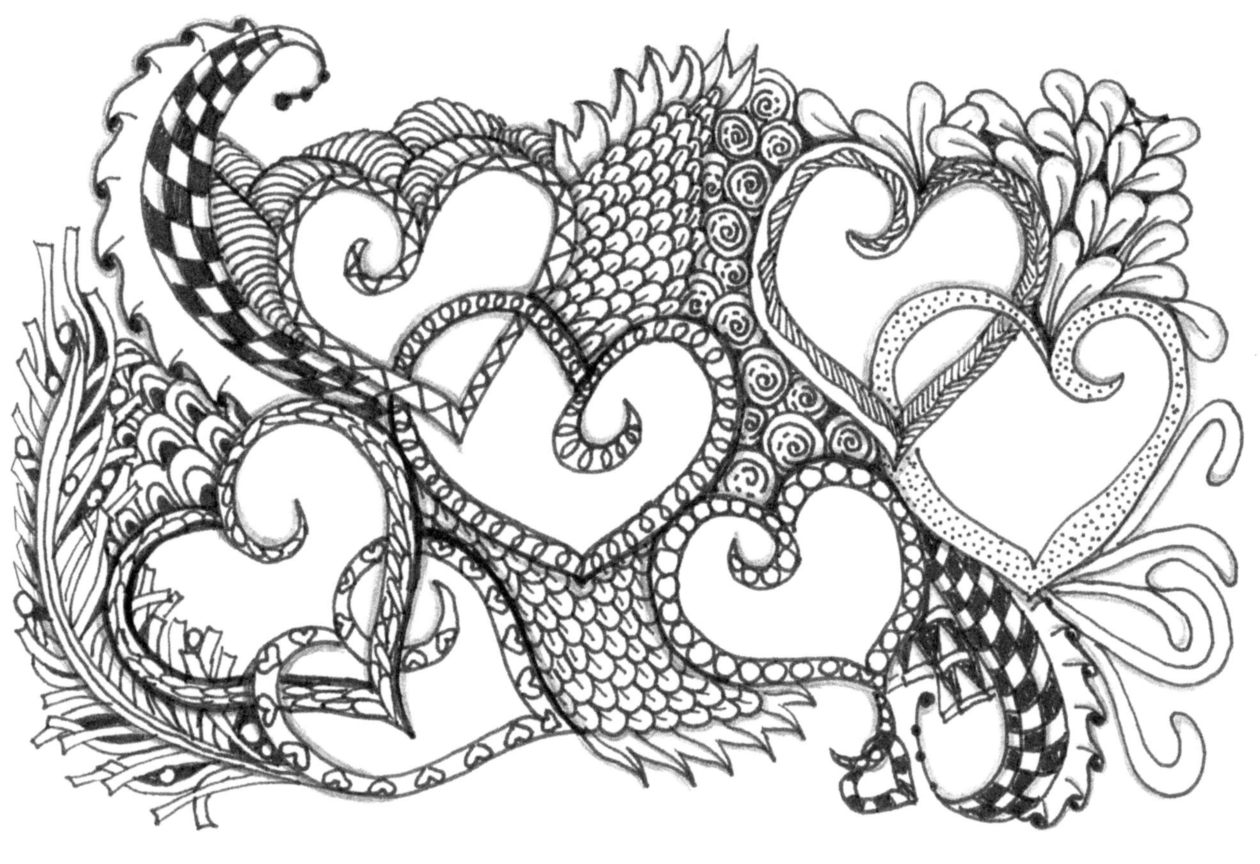

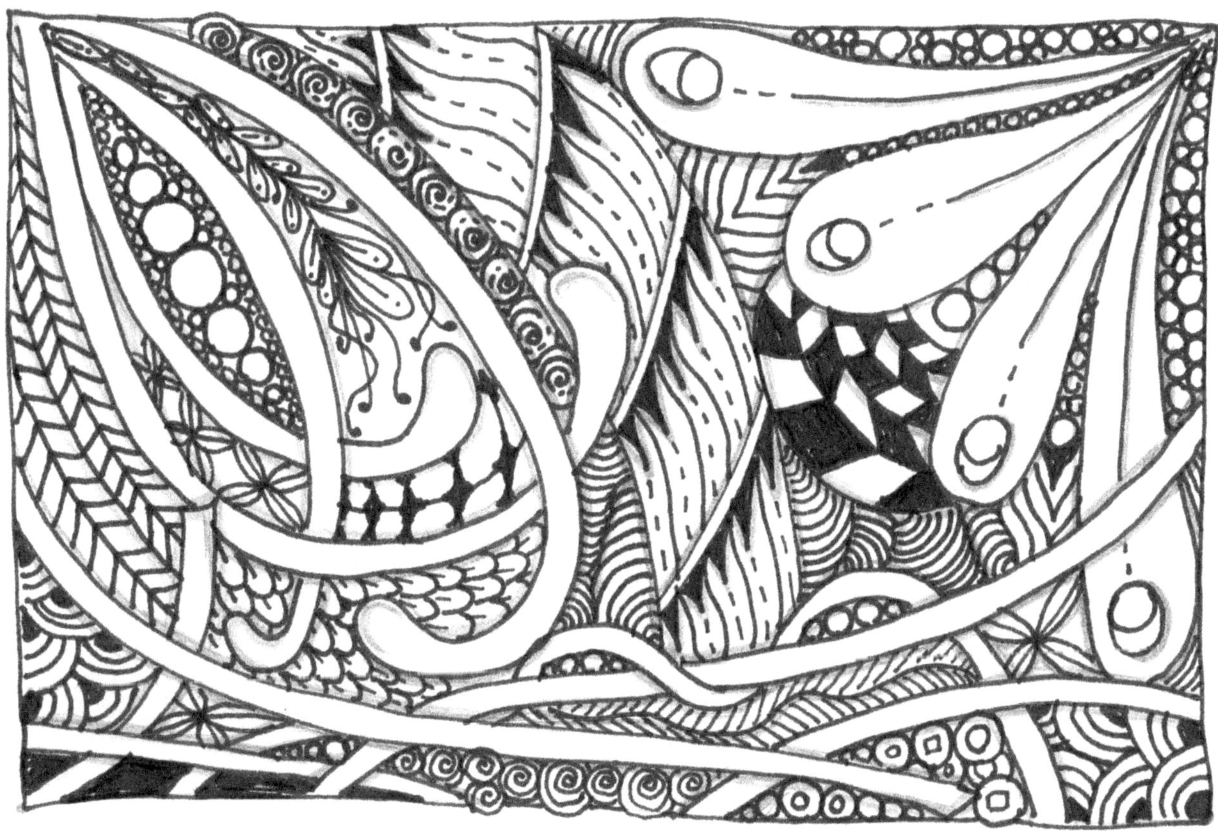

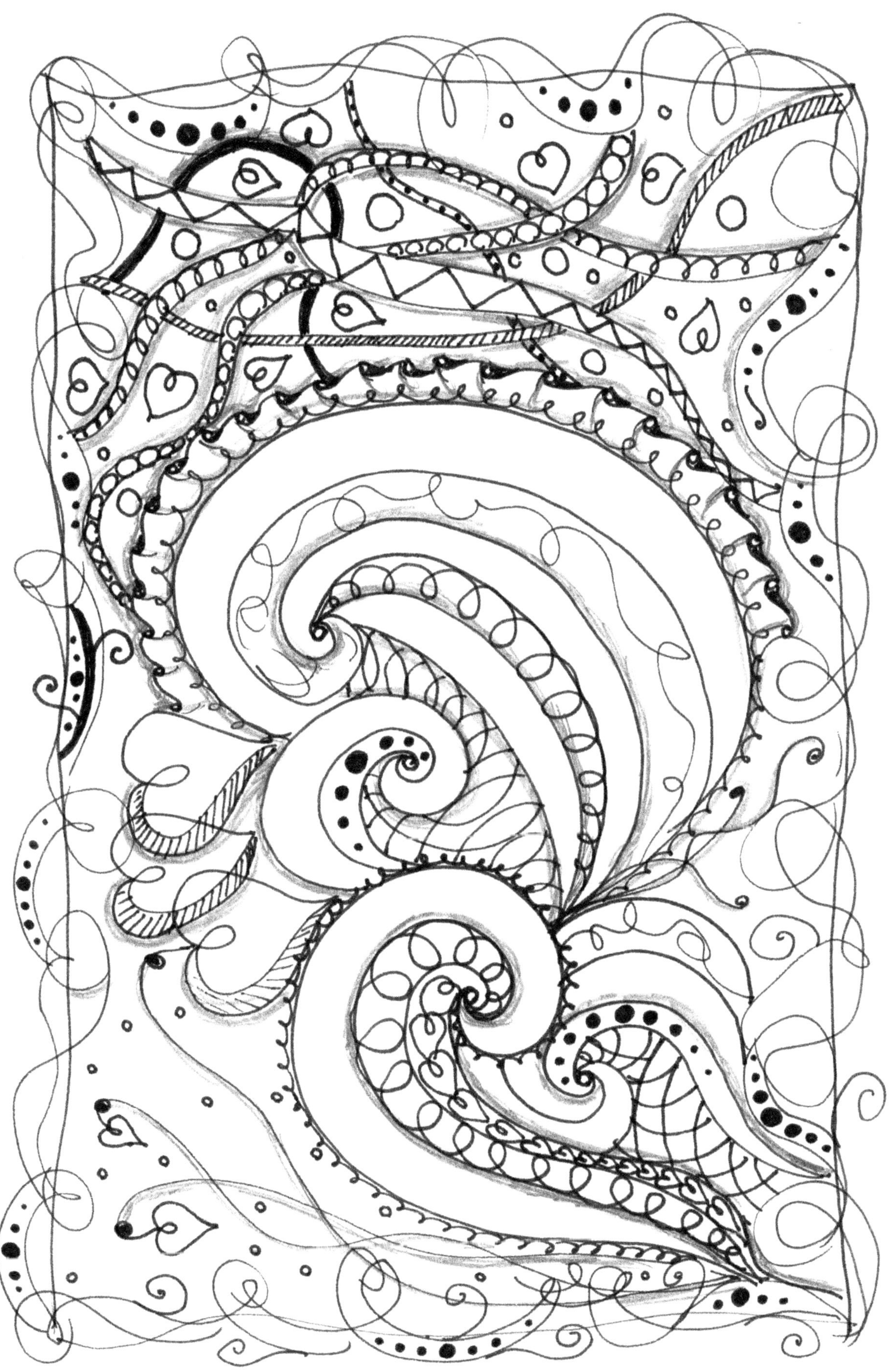

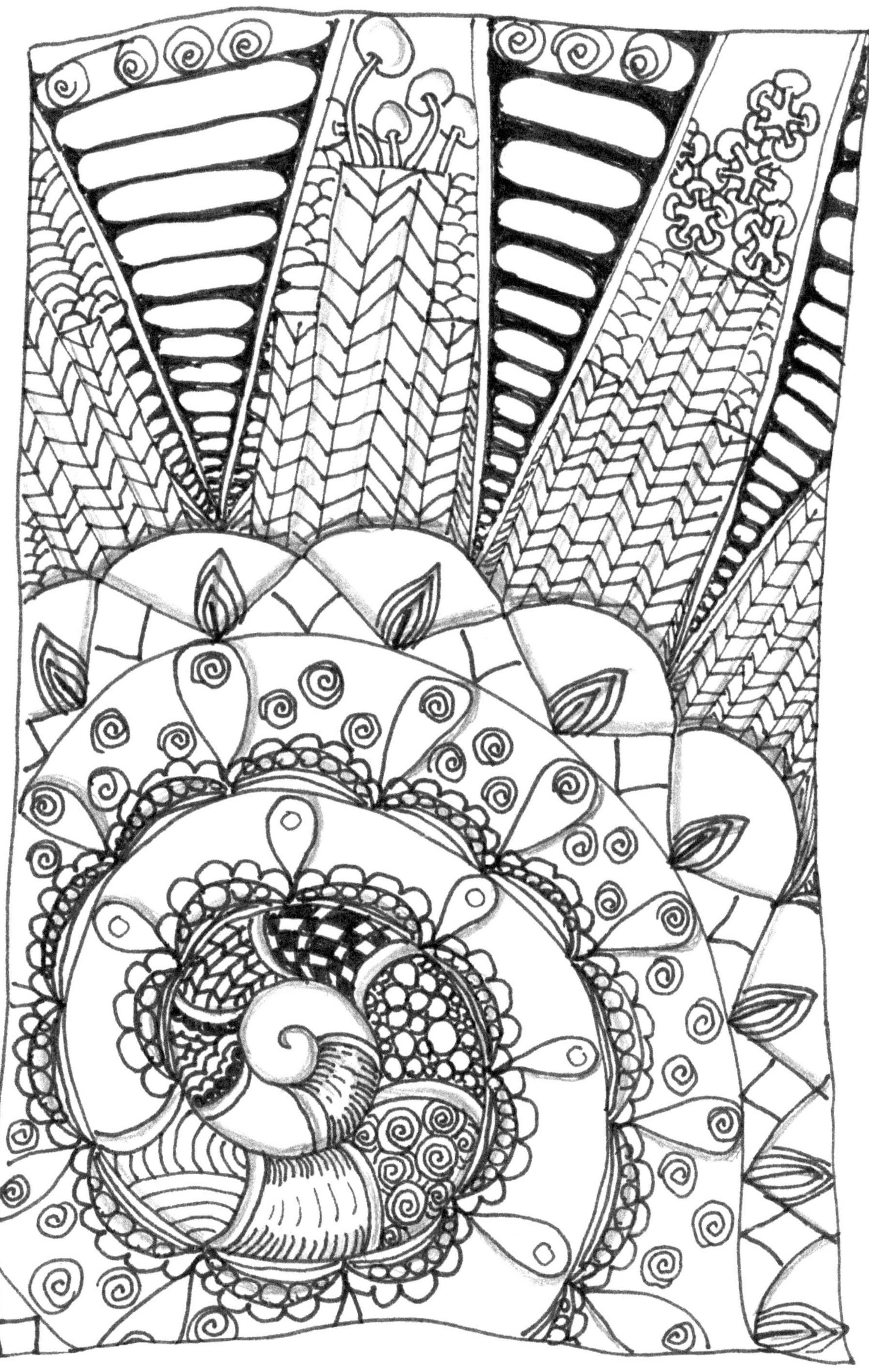

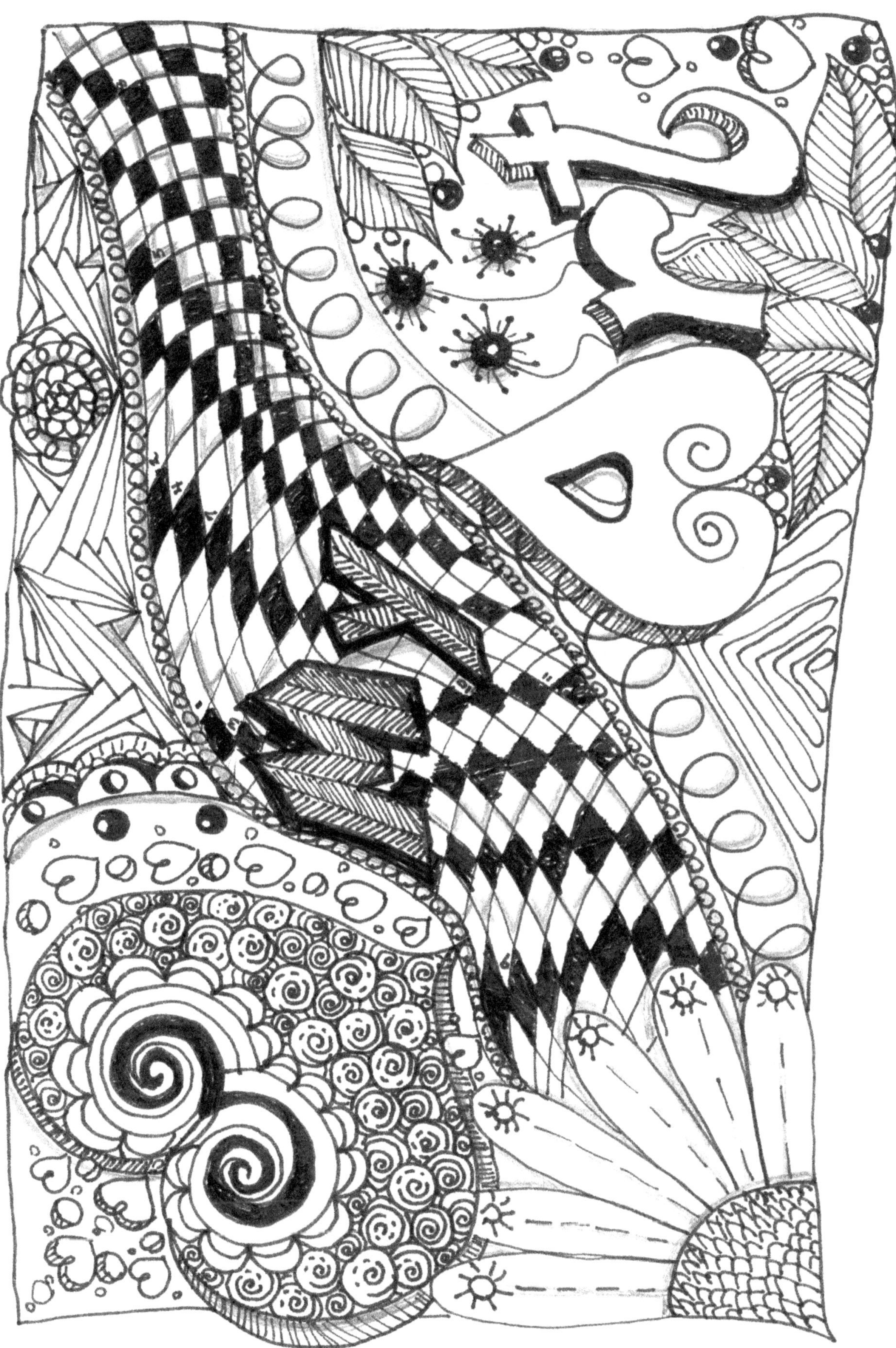

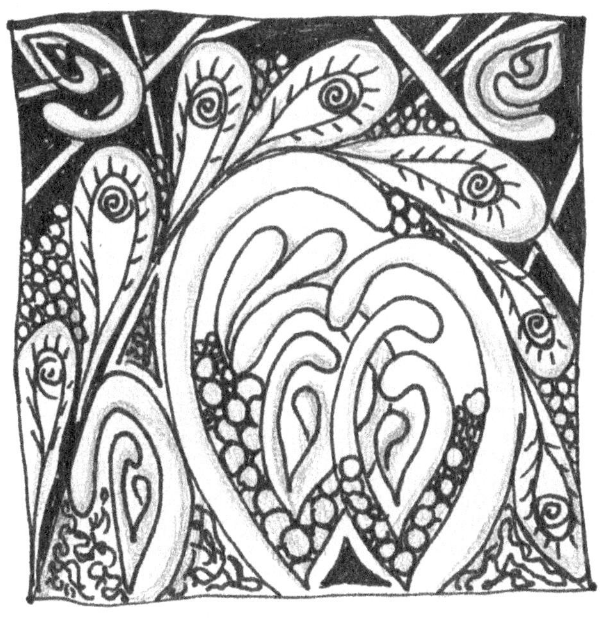

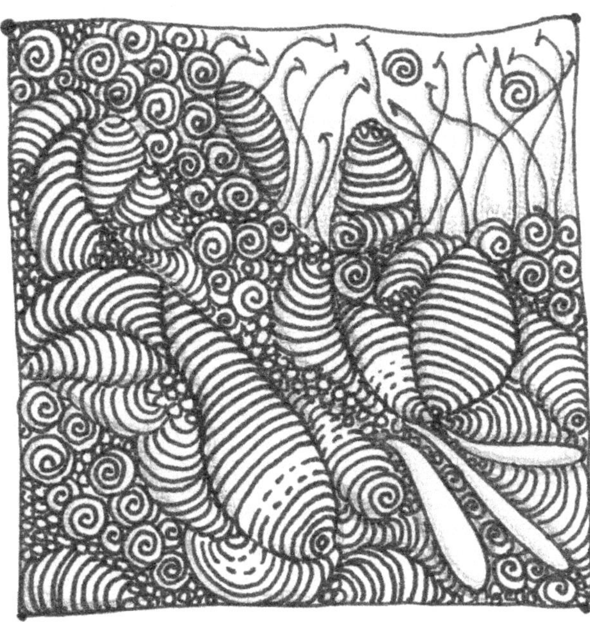

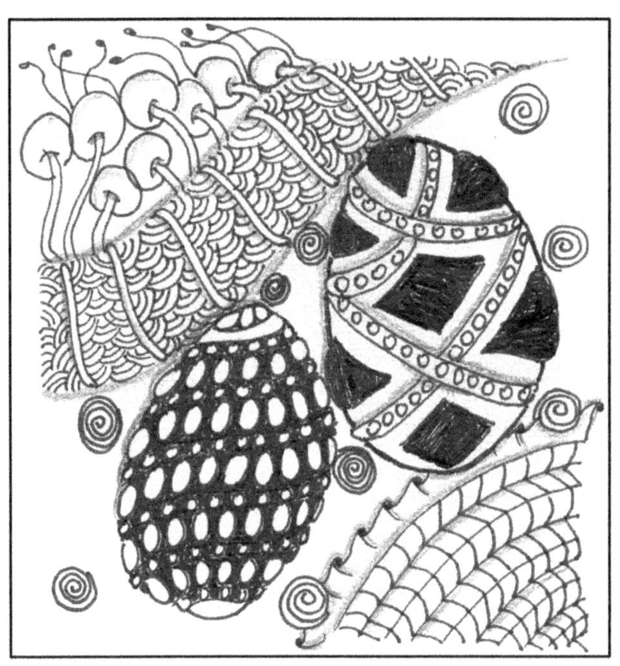

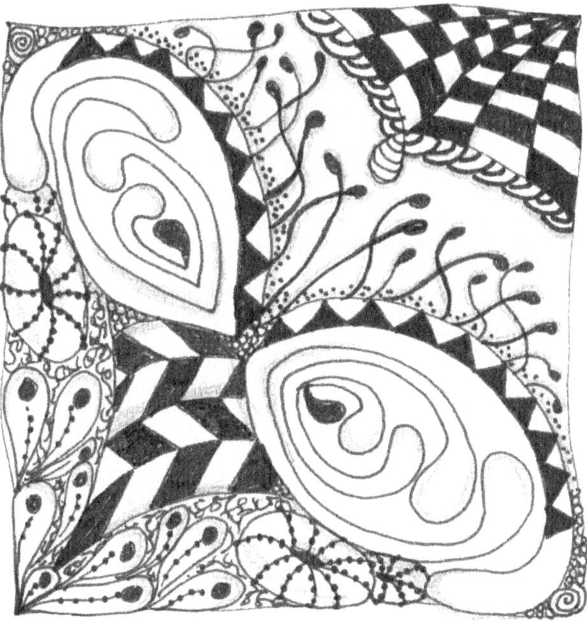

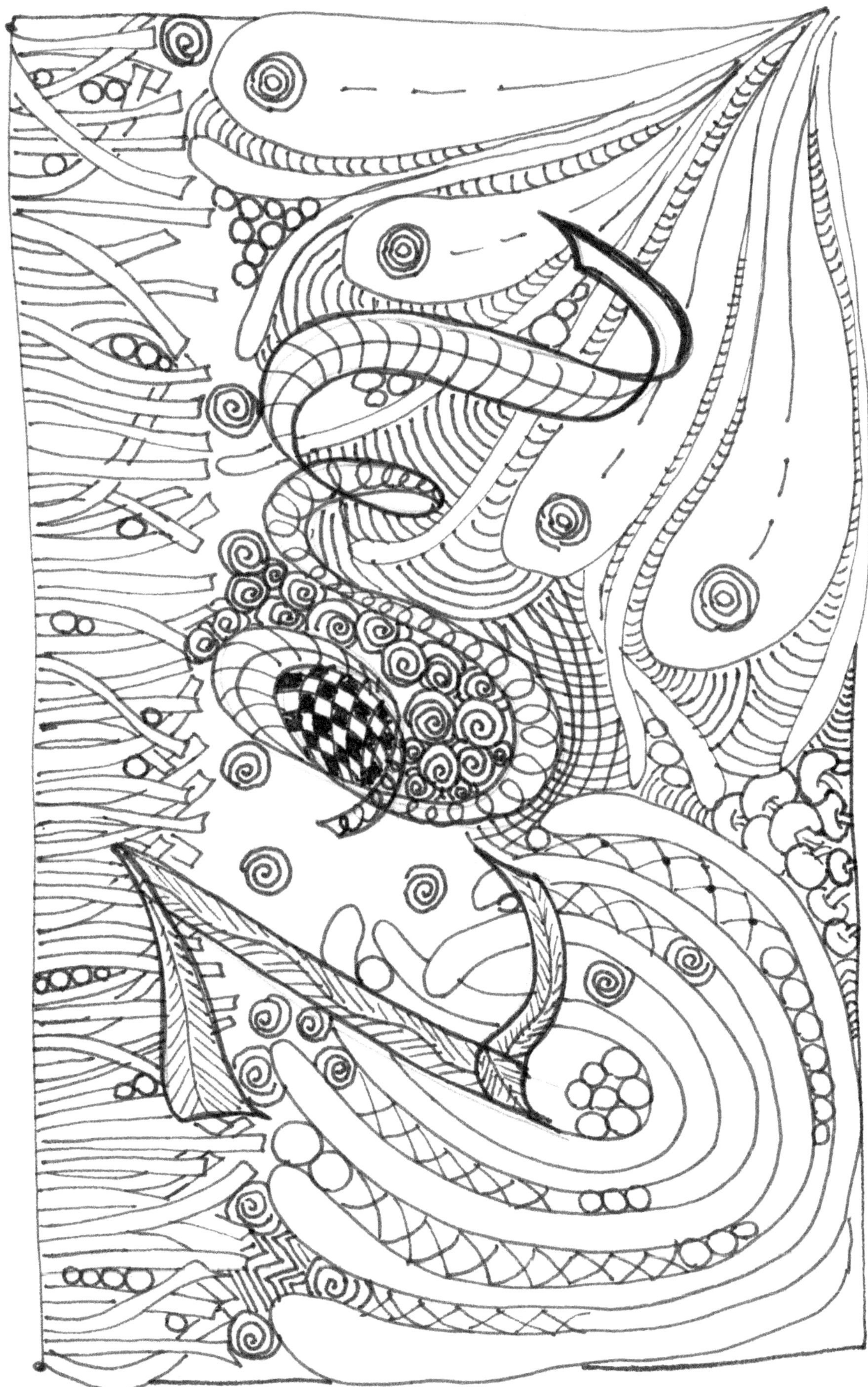

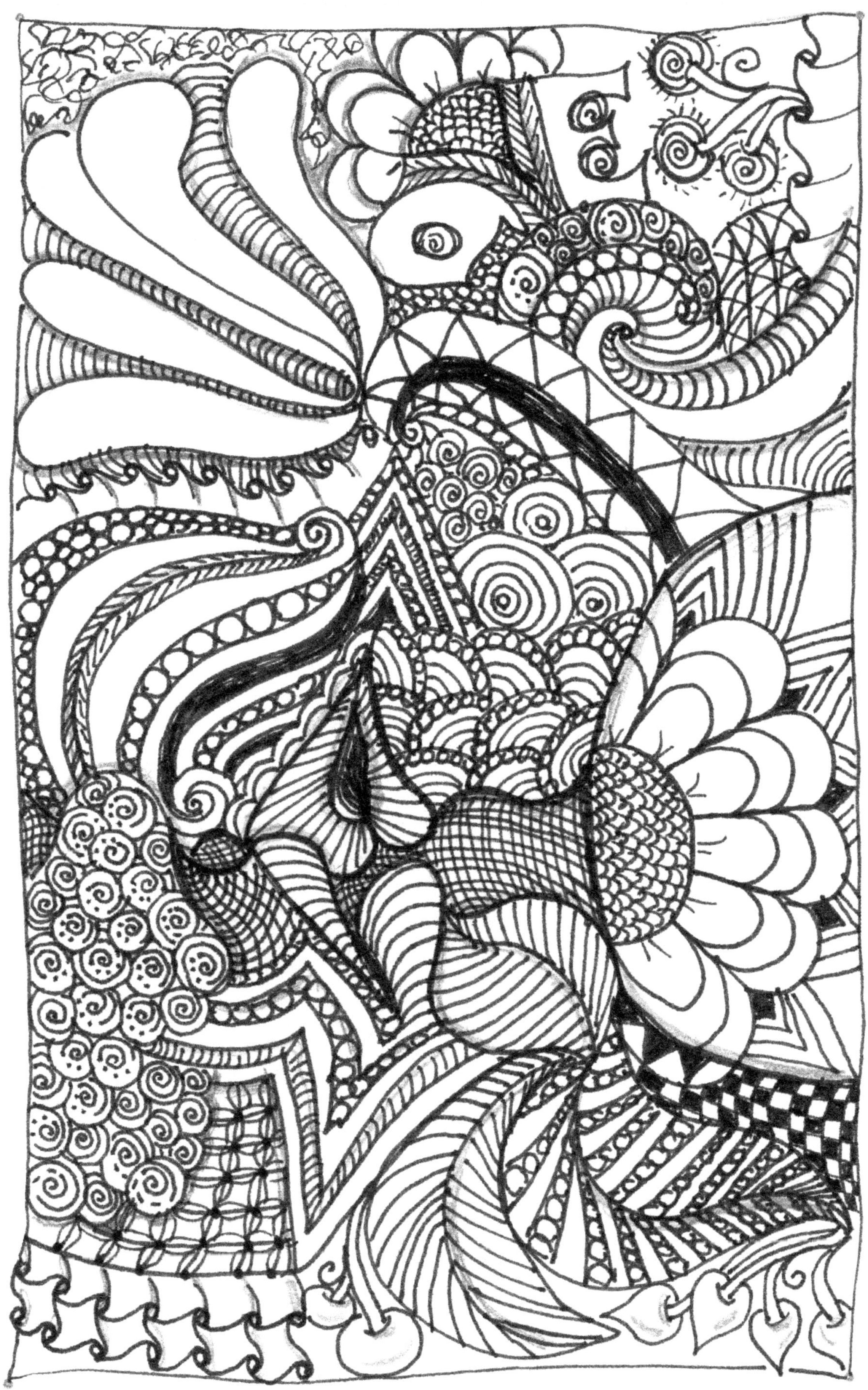

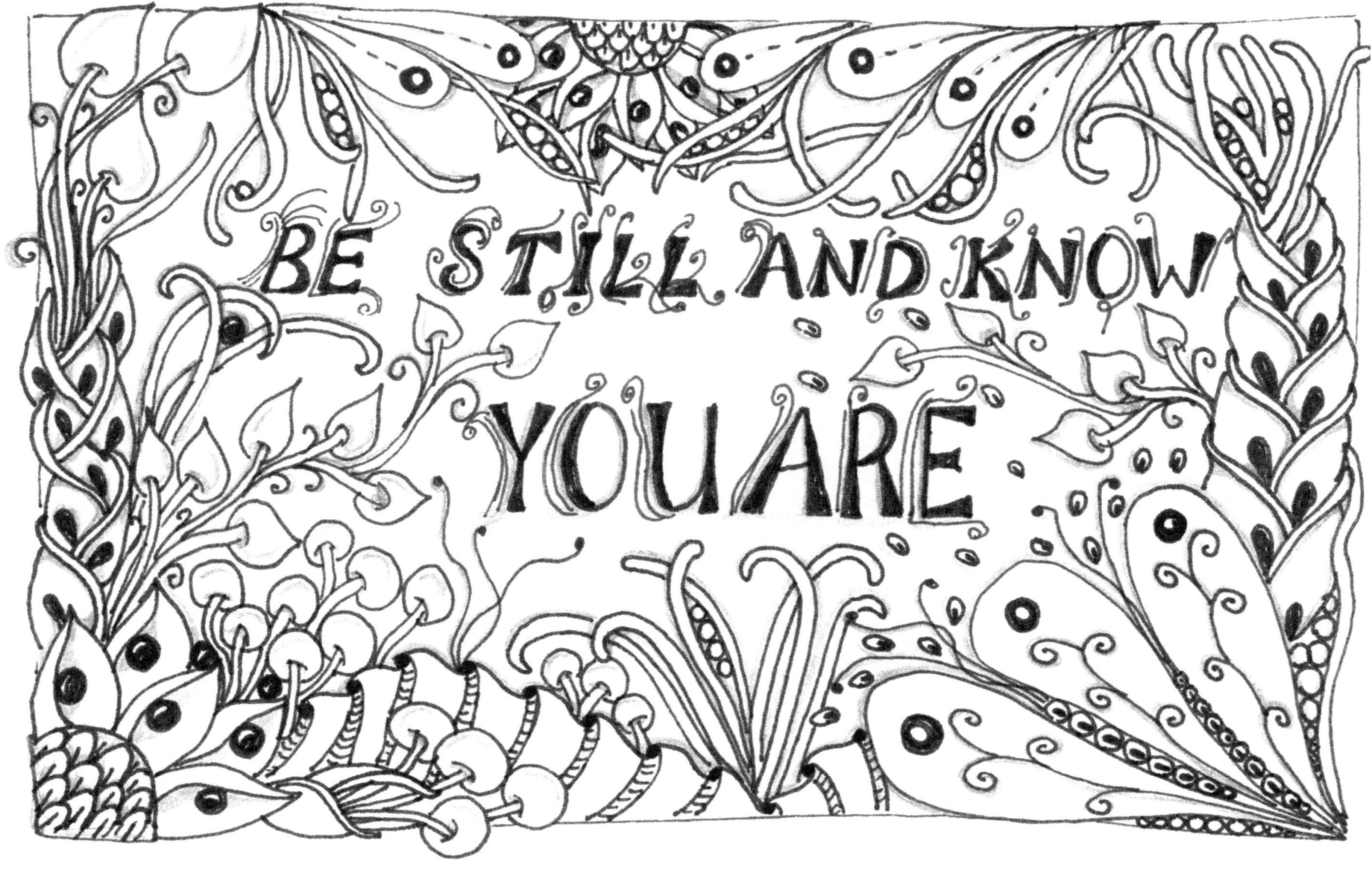
BE STILL AND KNOW
YOU ARE

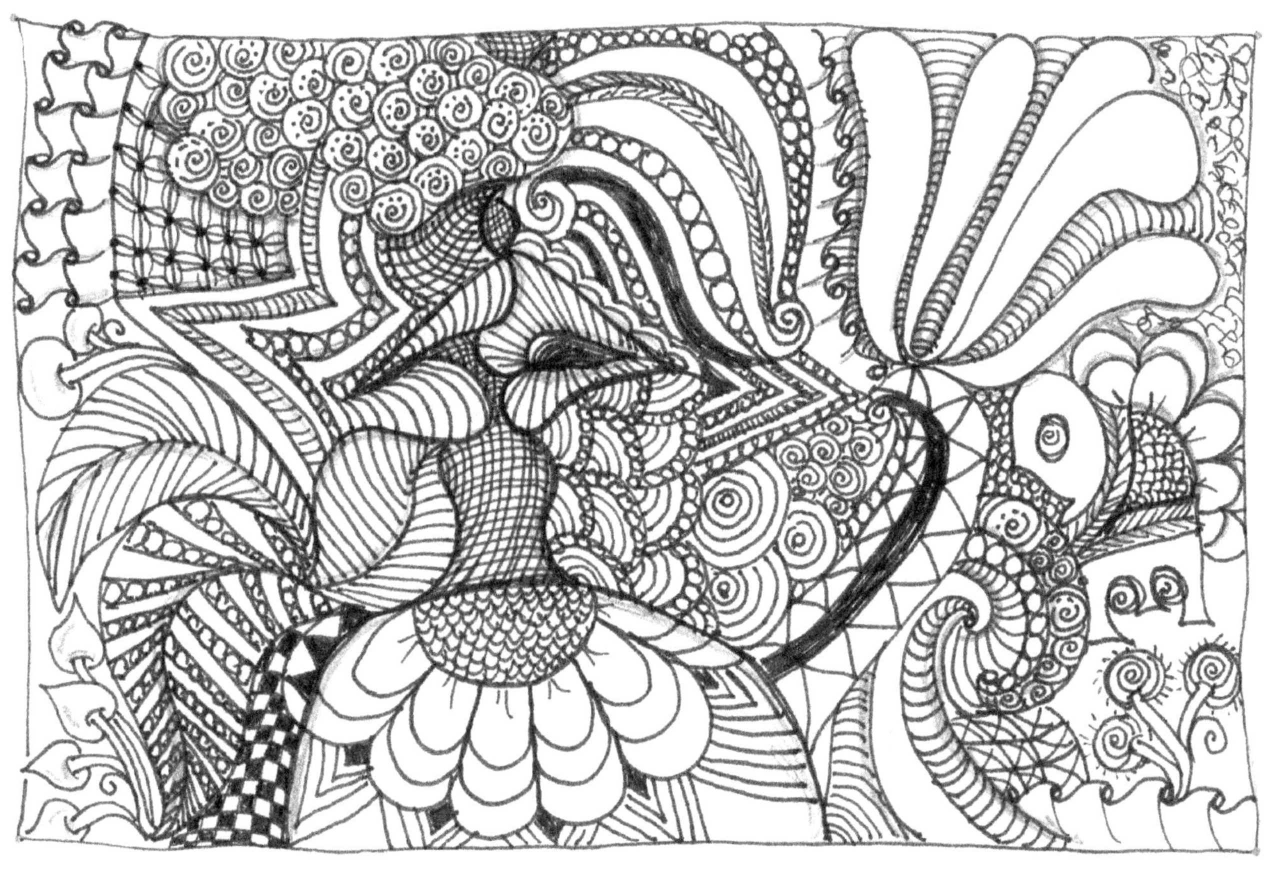

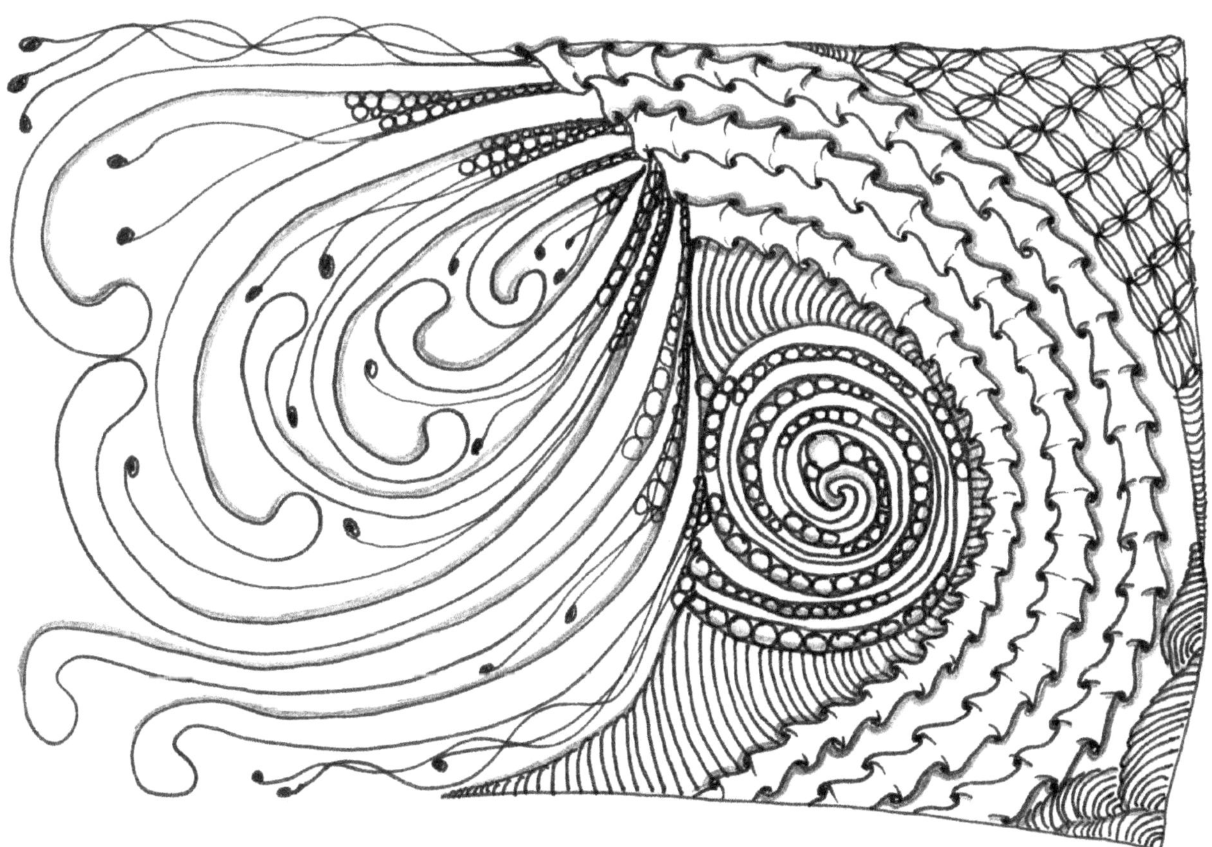

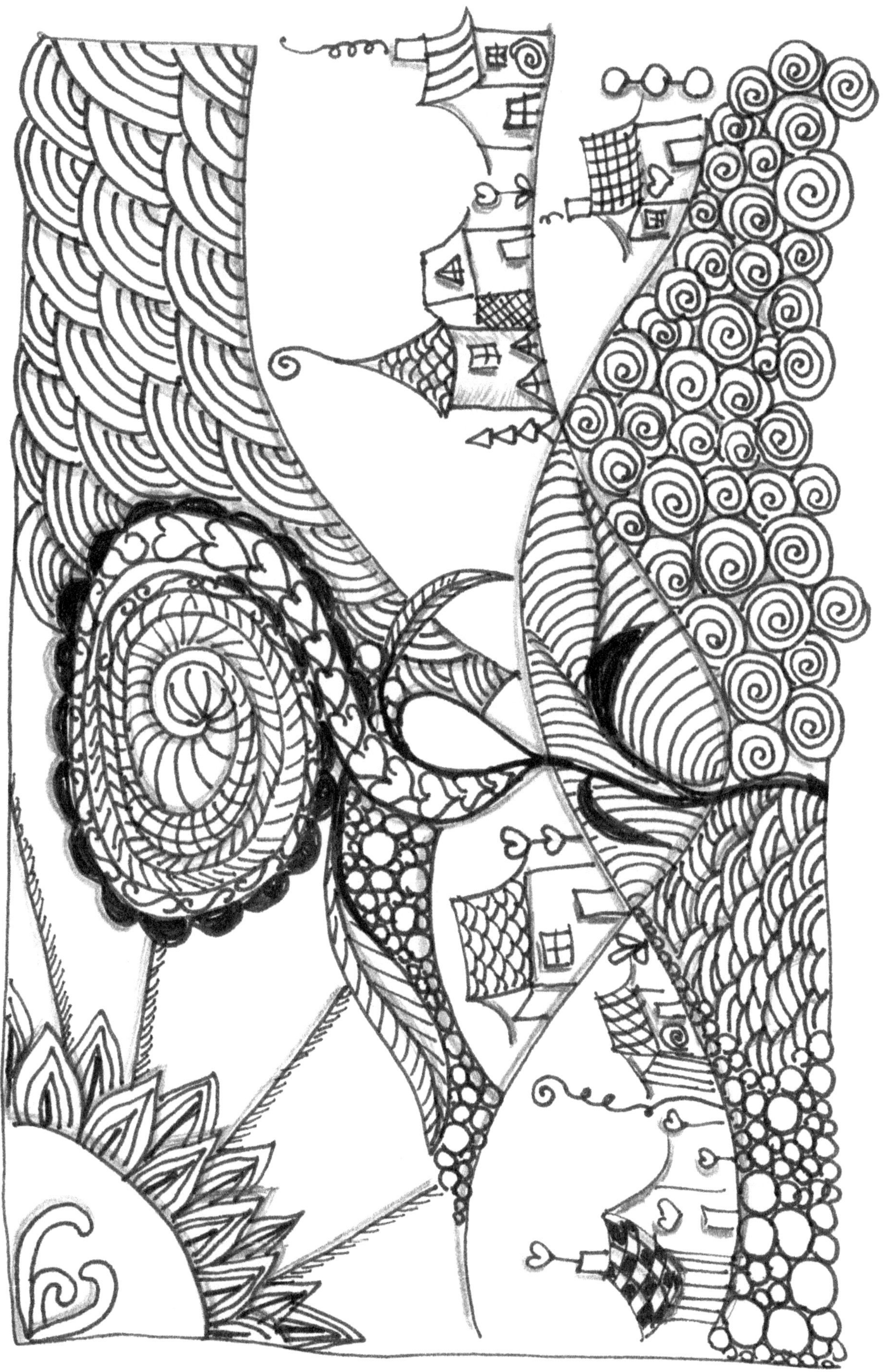

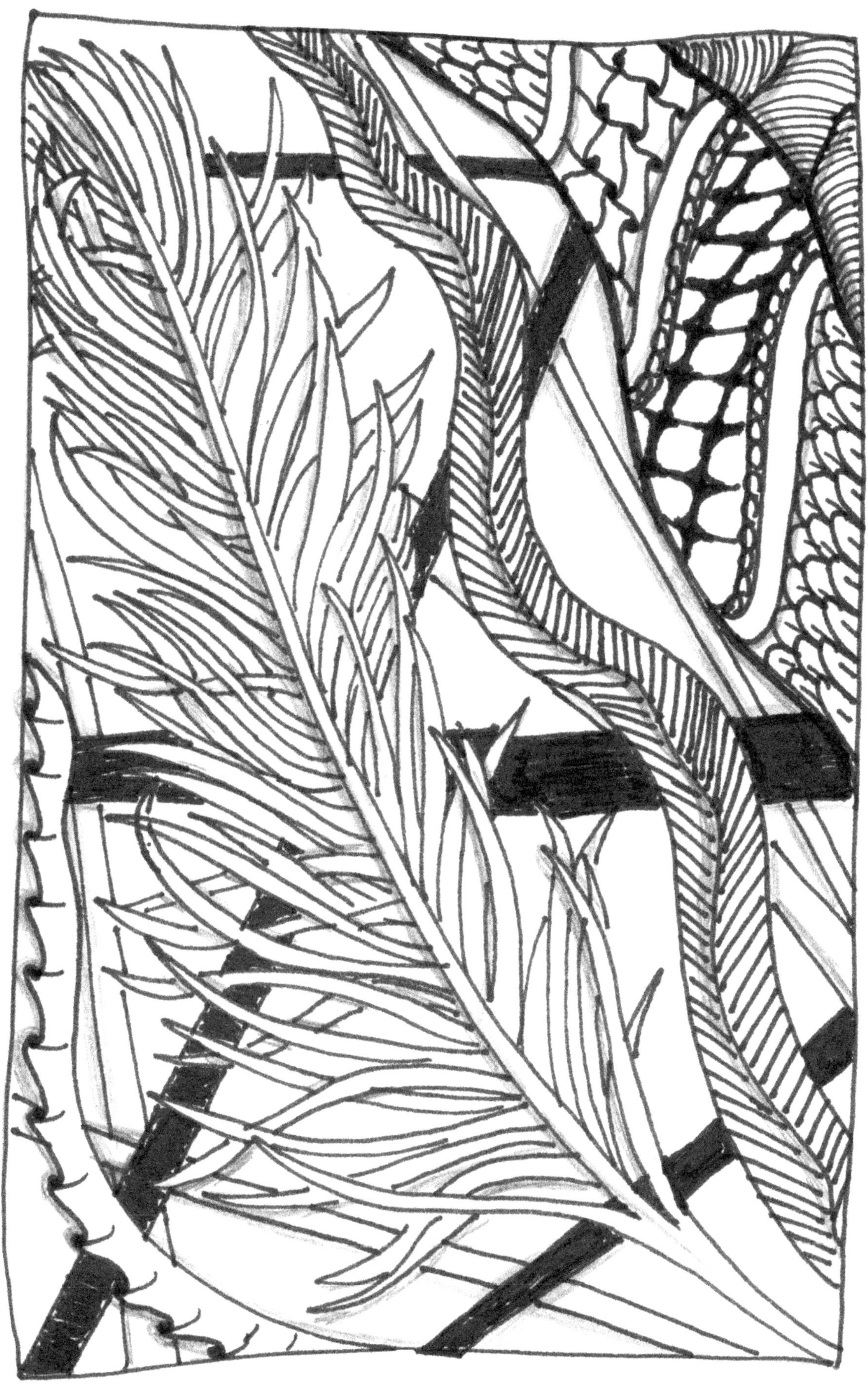

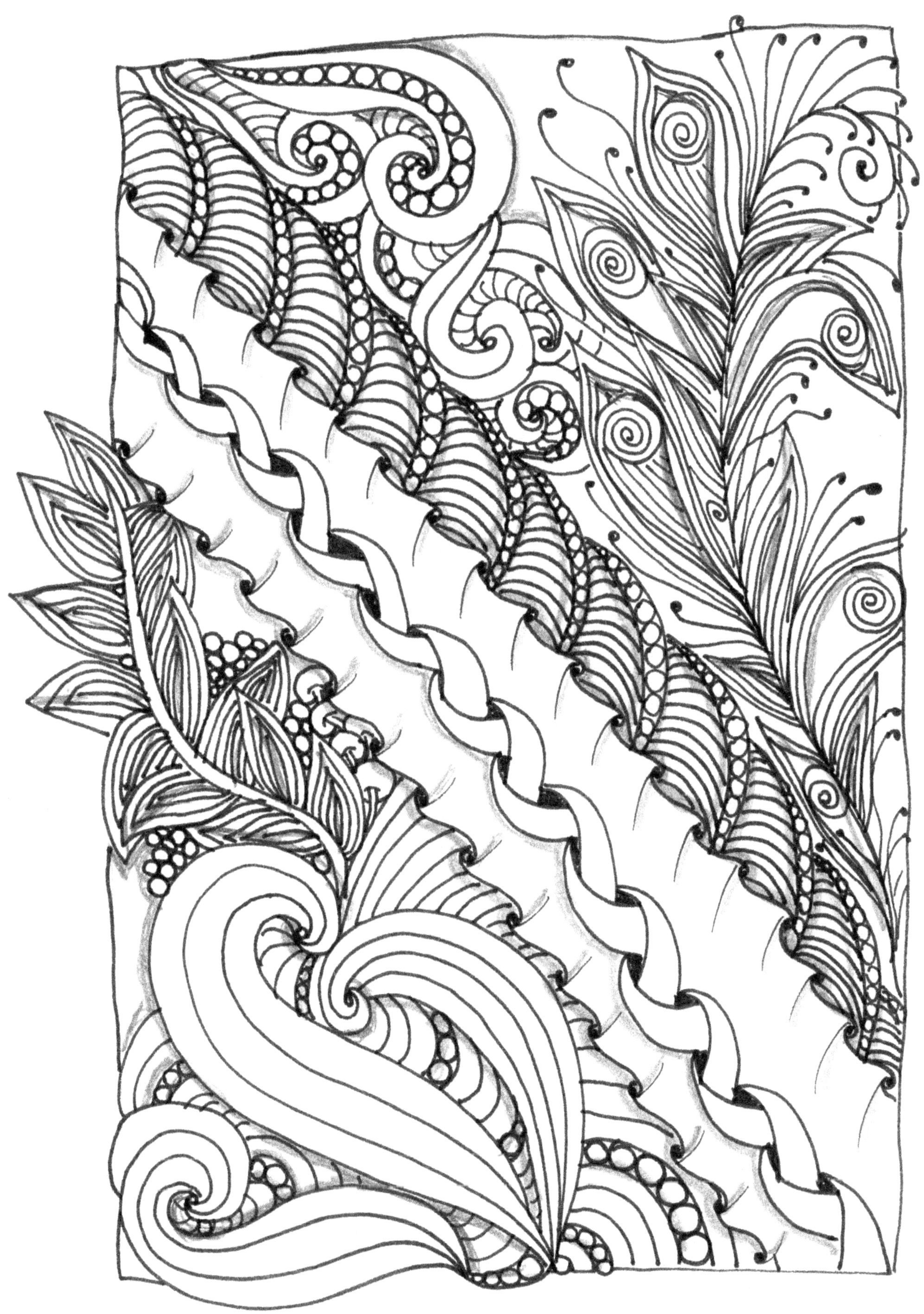

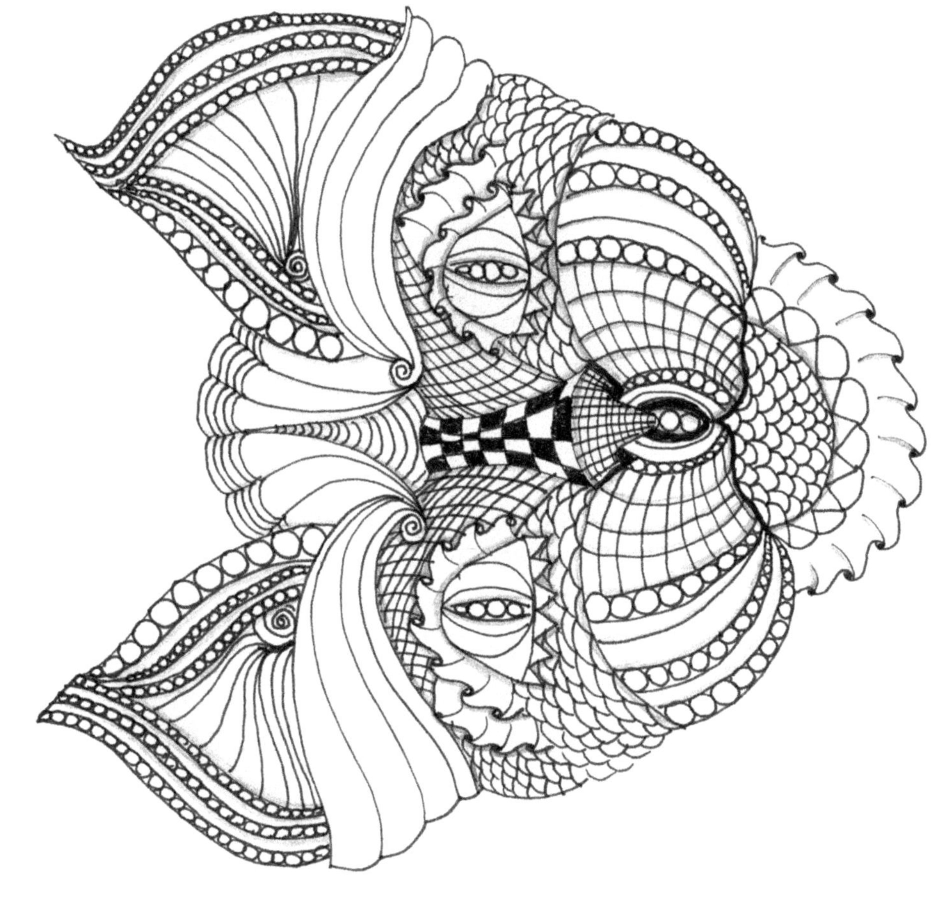

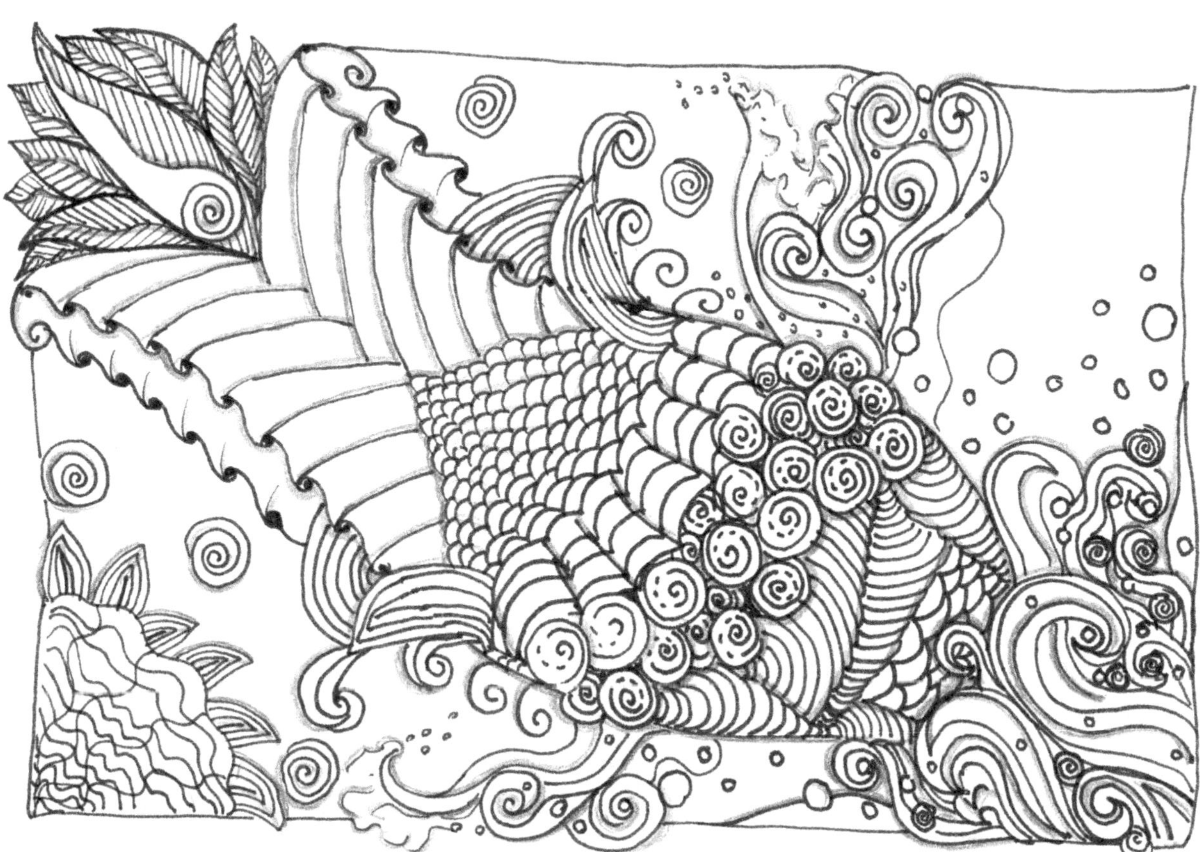

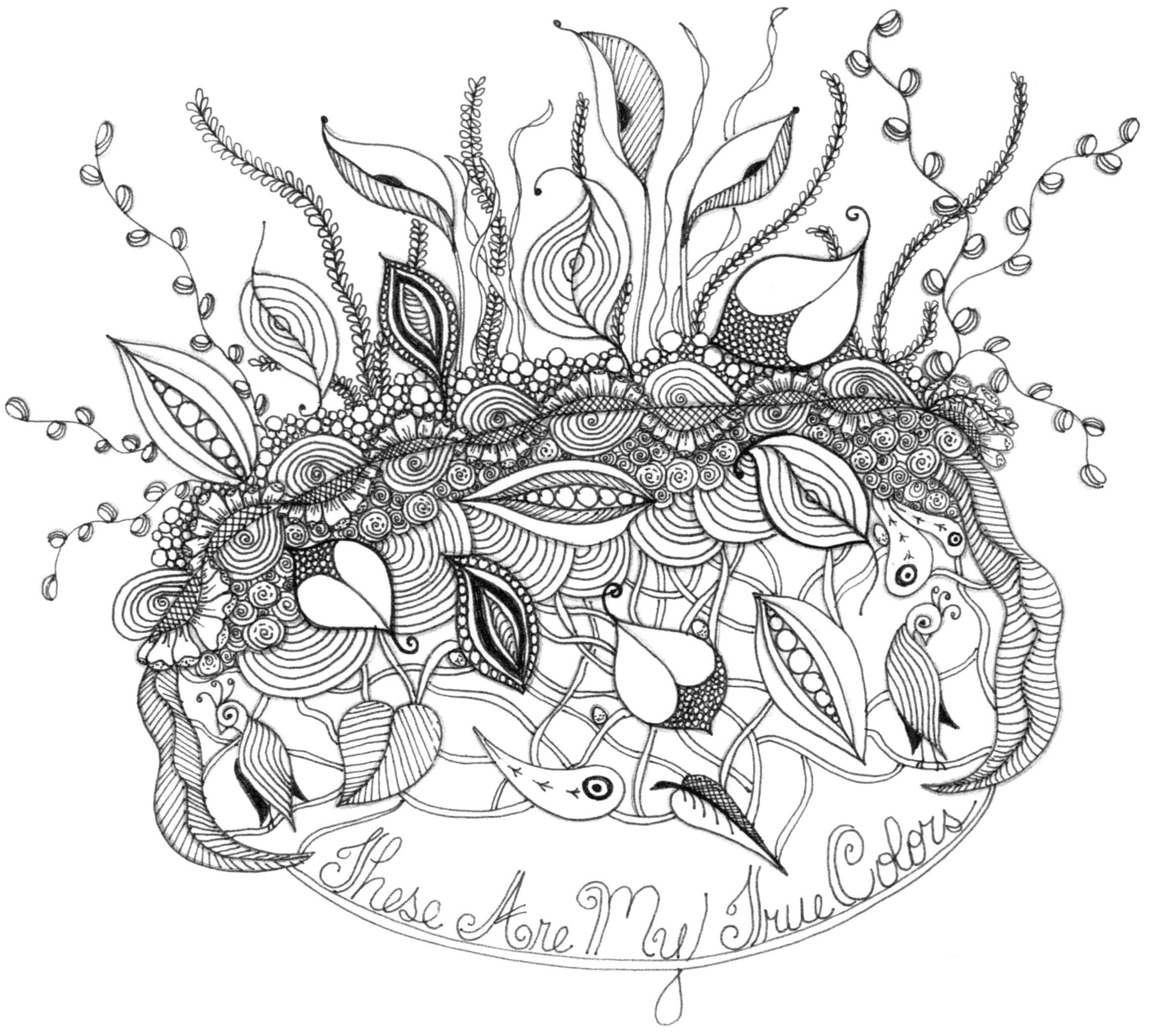
These Are My True Colors

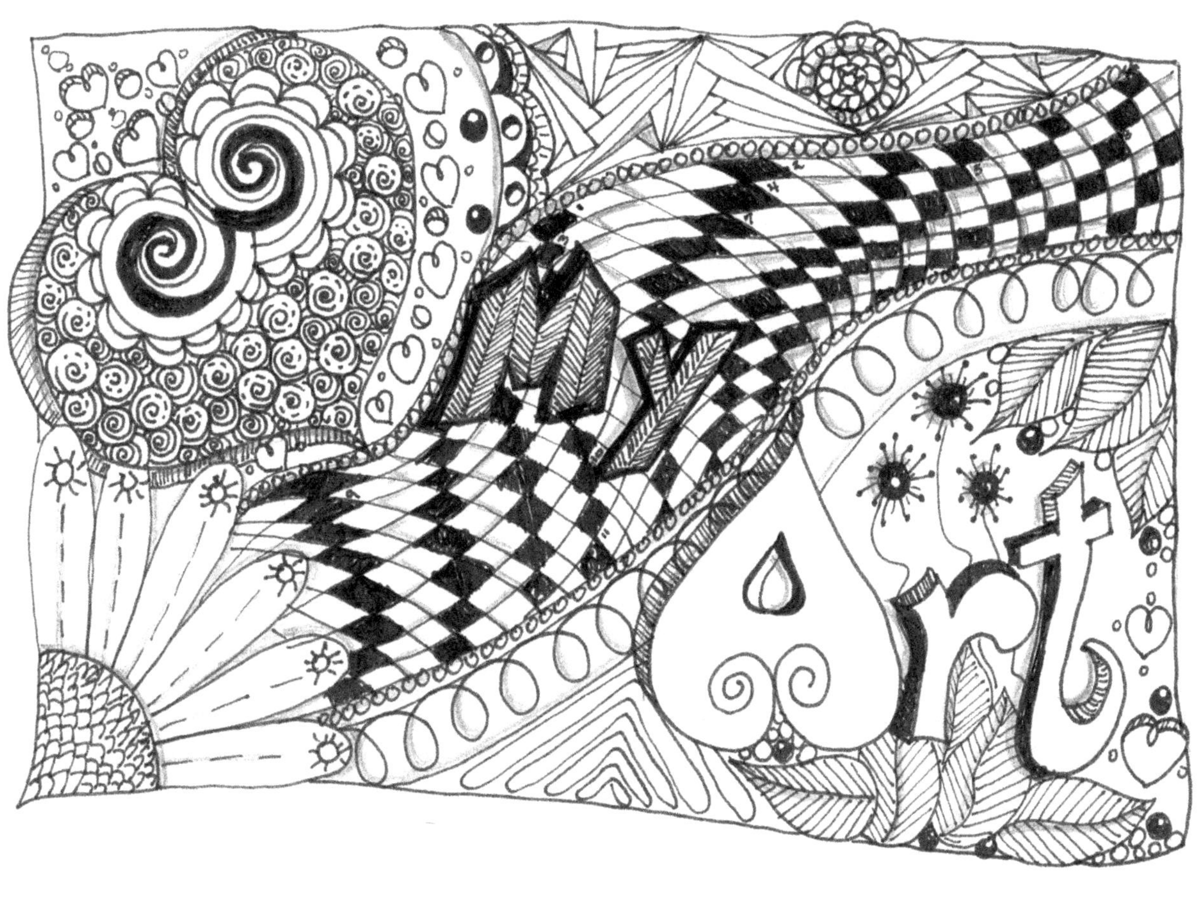
My
Art

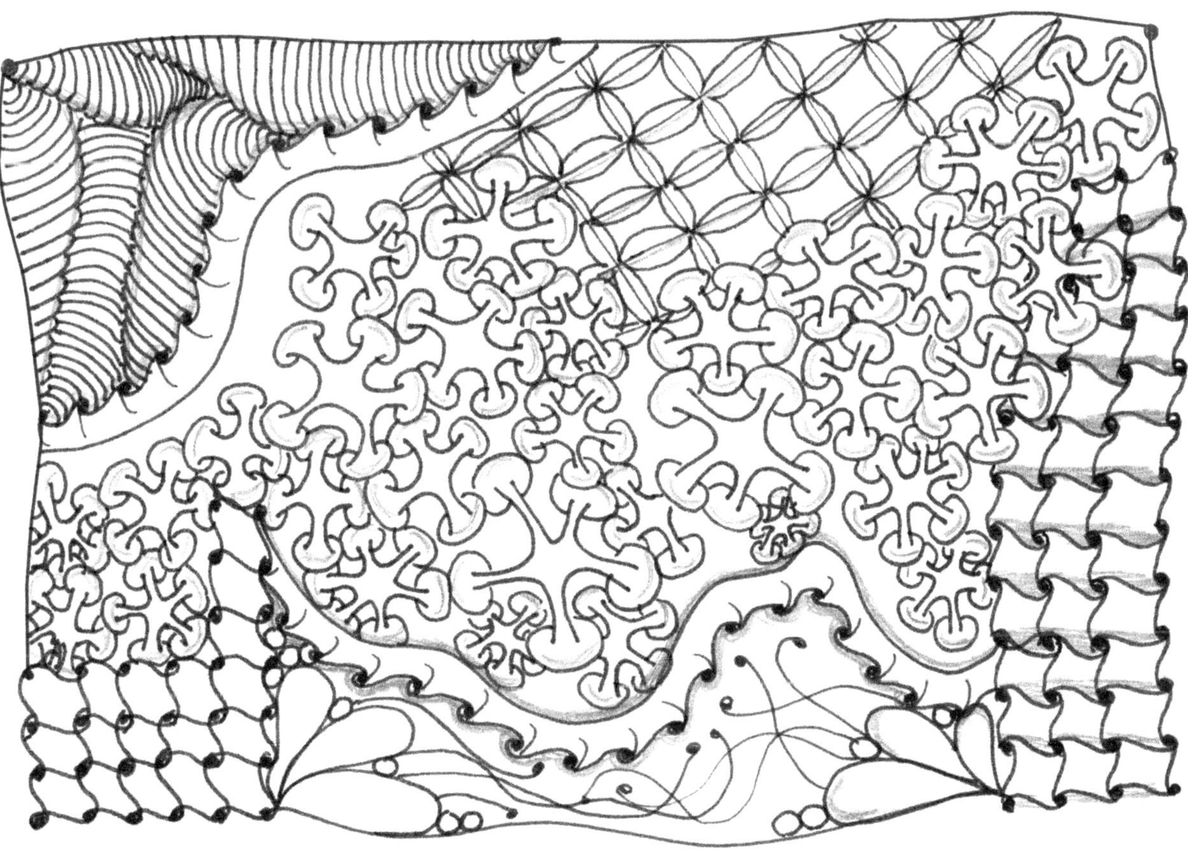

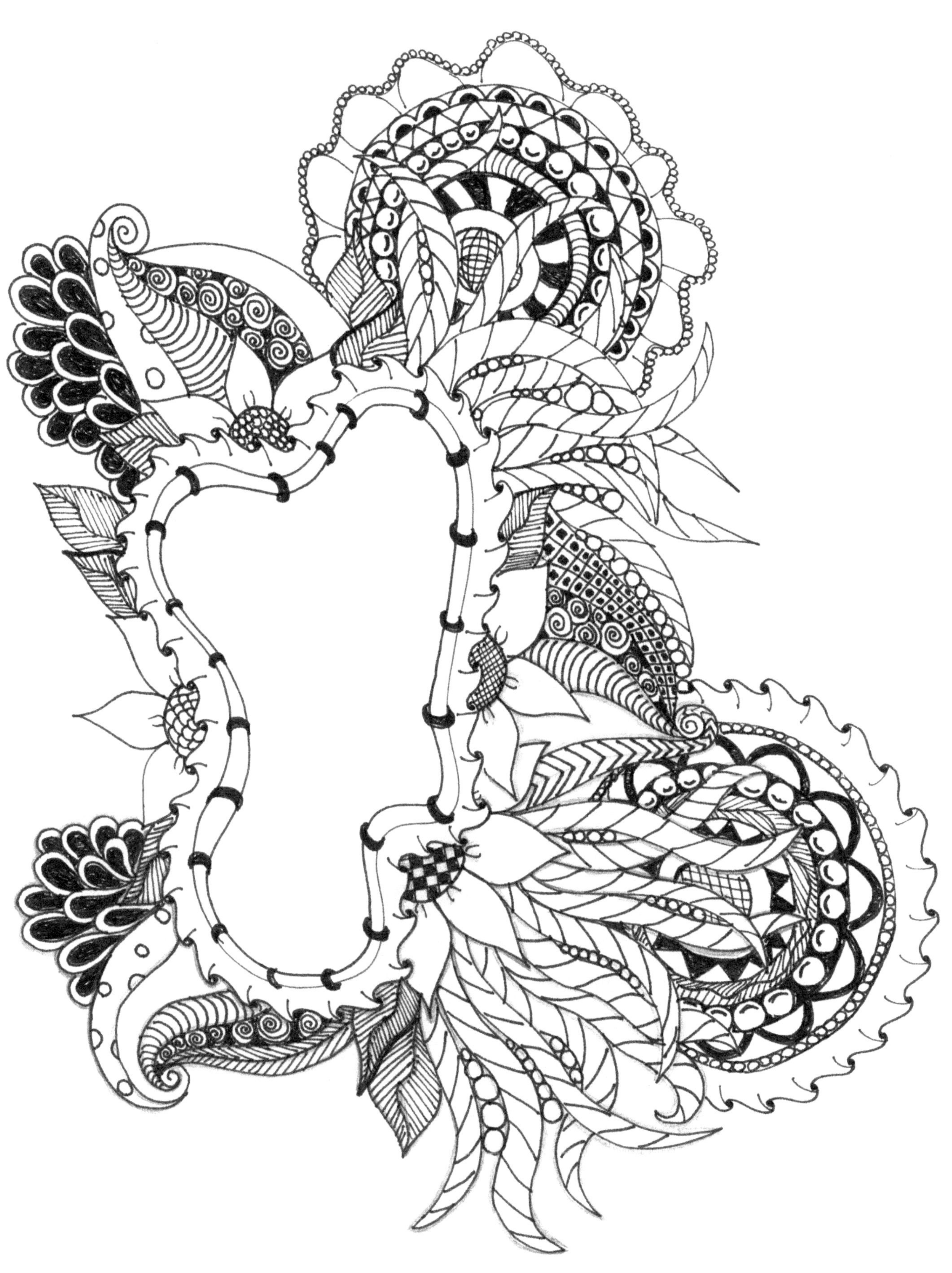

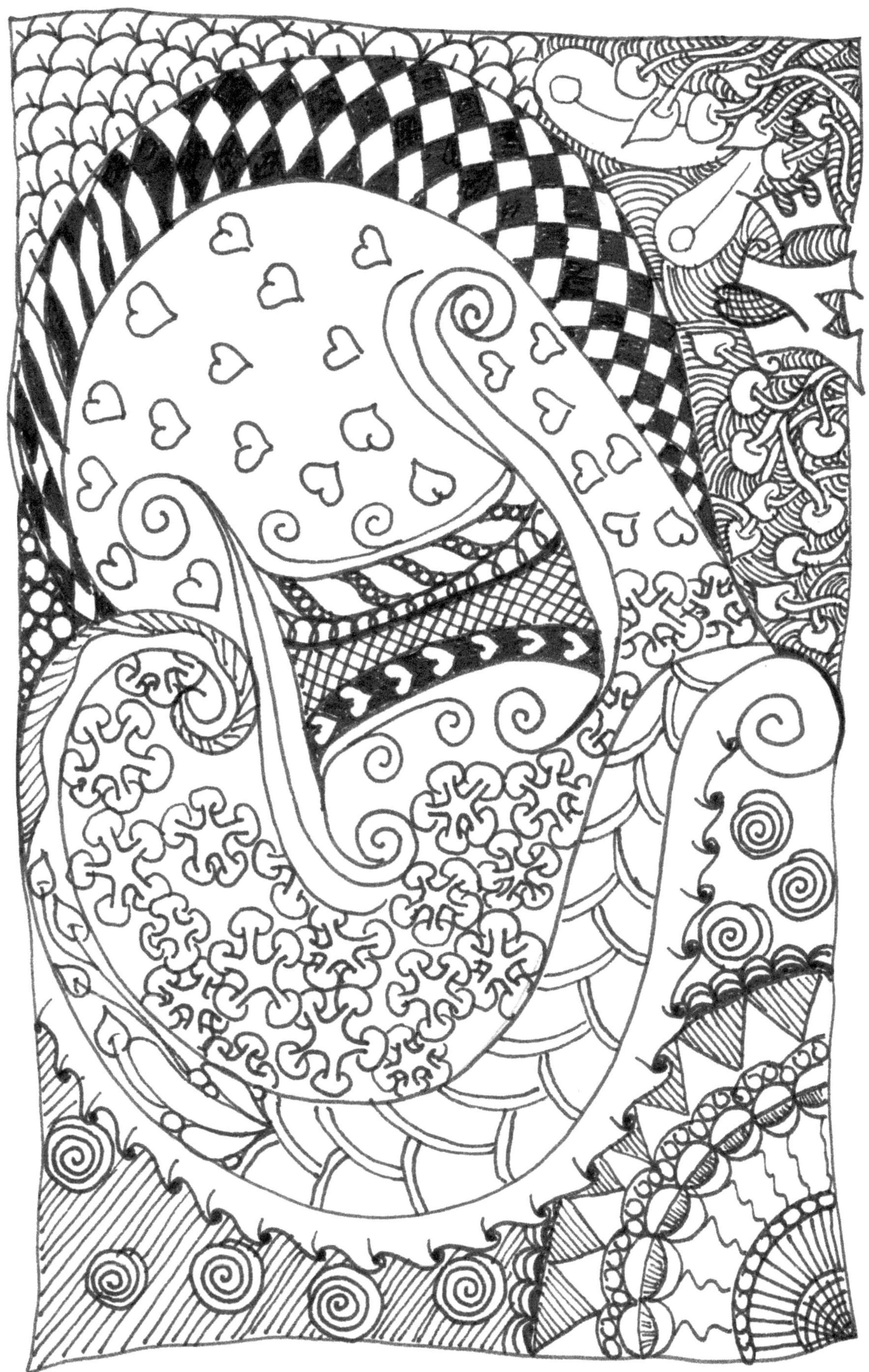

ABOUT THE ARTIST:

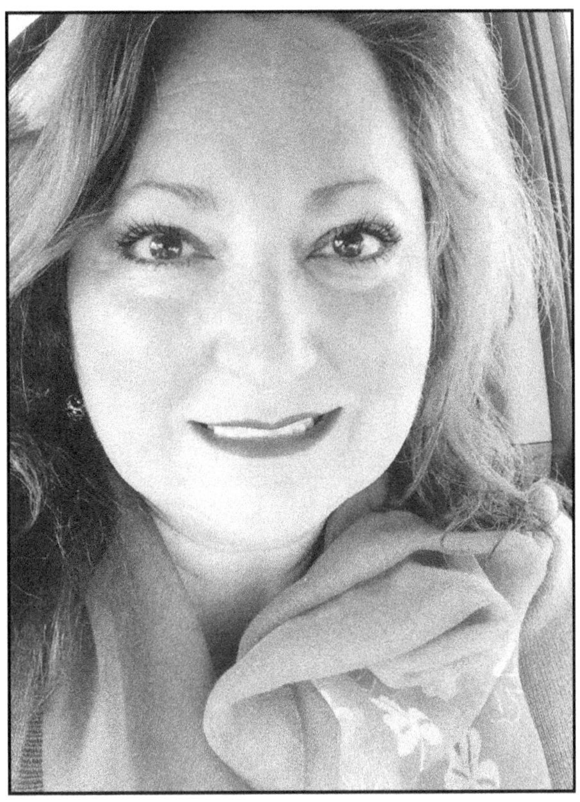

Cathy Lynn is a writer, facilitator, executive, and artist. She has been a featured columnist for two personal growth blogs, *3 Shared Paths* and *Women's Life Link*. She is co-owner of Inkwell Basics and is owner of The Barefoot Farm, a rustic event venue in the middle of Tennessee's largest Amish community.

She lives somewhere between the city and the country with her cats, Sebastian and Miss Kitty.

GET IN TOUCH WITH CATHY:

Email: cathylynnartist@gmail.com

Pinterest: pinterest.com/thebarefootfarm

Facebook: facebook.com/artistcathylynn

www.ingramcontent.com/pod-product-compliance
Lightning Source LLC
LaVergne TN
LVHW081410110826
845149LV00010B/1691

* 9 7 8 0 9 9 6 6 6 0 7 0 9 *